UN MARKETING

Stop Marketing. Start Engaging.

Revised
and Updated

Scott Stratten

WILEY

John Wiley & Sons, Inc.

Published by John Wiley & Sons, Inc., Hoboken, New Jersey.
Published simultaneously in Canada.

For general information on our other products and services or for technical support, please contact our Customer Care Department within the United States at (800) 762-2974, outside the United States at (317) 572-3993 or fax (317) 572-4002.

Wiley publishes in a variety of print and electronic formats and by print-on-demand. Some material included with standard print versions of this book may not be included in e-books or in print-on-demand. If this book refers to media such as a CD or DVD that is not included in the version you purchased, you may download this material at http://booksupport.wiley.com. For more information about Wiley products, visit www.wiley.com.

Library of Congress Cataloging-in-Publication Data:

Stratten, Scott.
 UnMarketing : stop marketing. Start engaging / Scott Stratten. — Rev. and updated.
   p. cm.
 ISBN: 978-1-118-17628-3 (pbk)
 ISBN: 978-1-118-28842-9 (ebk)
 ISBN: 978-1-118-28841-2 (ebk)
 ISBN: 978-1-118-28840-5 (ebk)
   1. Relationship marketing.   2. Viral marketing.   I. Title.
 HF5415.55.S76 2012
 658.8′02–dc23   2011042846

Printed in the United States of America

10 9 8 7 6 5 4 3

For UnJunior

Contents

Introduction

"GOOD AFTERNOON!"

It was the start of an exchange that would set off a chain of events that would shift my opinion of a billion-dollar establishment with one simple act. Let me explain. It's no secret I "enjoy" Las Vegas. After going there 15 times in the past four years, I consider myself an unofficial tour guide and resident of Sin City.

A place that you definitely cannot miss on the strip is the Wynn—very fancy, very pretty, and very expensive. Because the place cost $2.7 billion to build, I assume selling 99-cent hot dogs isn't going to make that money back. I really didn't care about the Wynn—not in a negative way, it just wasn't on my radar. After getting comfortable staying at MGM Grand, The Venetian, and other places, I didn't really see a need to change, until that Saturday.

I had a meeting at the Wynn during the BlogWorld conference. I strolled in through the majestic doors with a friend of mine. As soon as we walked in, we spotted a man (Wes) using a large carpet-cleaning machine. He wasn't in our way, so we really thought nothing of it, but he thought differently. He stopped what he was doing. He looked up and smiled. Not one of those "it's part of my job to smile" ones, but a genuine, warm, authentic smile.

And then he said, "Good afternoon, and welcome to the Wynn, please enjoy your day," all the while looking us right in the eye, like it was his mission to ensure that we knew he meant business.

His welcome changed my entire perception of the Wynn. Almost $3 billion went into making this megacasino resort, and it was one guy who made me want to stay there. He made me want to tell the world about it—made me want to blog about it. The carpet-cleaning dude. I have passed hundreds of people cleaning in casinos in Vegas, but I've rarely been given eye contact, and not once felt welcomed. As a matter of fact, I have never, ever been greeted like that by anyone in Vegas. It is wonderful and sad at the same time. This gentleman, who made me feel welcome at his place of employment, was not only exceptional, but he was extremely rare.

Casinos (and probably most of you in business) all have the same stuff for the most part. All accountants offer accounting services, all coffee joints serve coffee, and all five-star resorts have fancy smells, spas, and pretty patterns. But only one resort has Wes.

Marketing is not a task.

Marketing is not a department.

Marketing is not a job.

Marketing happens every time you engage (or not) with your past, present, and potential customers. UnMarketing also takes it one step further—it is any time anyone talks about your company. Word of mouth is not a project or a viral marketing ploy. The mouths are already moving. You need to decide if you want to be a part of the conversation, which is why I call it UnMarketing—the ability to engage with your market. Whether you employ thousands or are a one-person show, you are always UnMarketing. It's what comes naturally, not being forced to do things that make you ill.[1] It's authentic, it's personal, and it's the way to build lifelong fans, relationships, and customers.

---

[1] *Cough* cold calling *cough*

> If you believe business is built on relationships, make building them your business.

That's the one line that you need to believe to UnMarket. If you don't believe that, return the book. Trash-talk me on Twitter.[2] Tell me that cold calling is a great tool if you know how to do it right. Just put the book down.

If you don't believe that your business is to build relationships, then tell me that the foundations of some of the greatest businesses in the world were built through cold calling. What worked decades ago does not work as well today, if at all. Getting a 0.2 percent return on your direct mail piece isn't cutting it anymore. Placing an ad multiple times in a newspaper[3] because "people have to see something seven times before acting" is a crock.[4] You need to return this book if you say, "I don't have time to build relationships online!" and yet will drive 45 minutes to a networking event, stay three hours, and drive 45 minutes back home.

You need to read this book if you've had enough of the old-school ways of marketing and want to believe there is a better way. You are the person who wants to believe that if you are your authentic self, you have no competition. That even though you may have thousands of providers in your industry to compete with, you bring unique things to the table (which you do).

Let's focus on building relationships and still building a business instead of throwing aside those who don't want to buy (Buy or Good-bye) and build lifelong relationships and a

---

[2] I'm @UnMarketing, just FYI for a place to point your insults.

[3] For those reading this in 2020, newspapers were things that used to be delivered door-to-door by kids initially, then by creepy dudes in vans at 4 AM. They were pages of ads with a sprinkle of articles. I know, weird, eh?

[4] I think that phrase was made up by an advertising sales rep. Brilliant.

profitable lifelong business, today. Being authentic has nothing to do with being cheesy or passive, and you don't have to sing "We Are the World" and hold hands. Being authentic means that you focus on what you bring to the table. That is what separates you from others in your industry. If you are your authentic self, then you have no competition. I know you have been told to act like other people, talk like other people, and market like all the people, but it is time that you unlearned everything and started to UnMarket yourself.

UN
MARKETING

1

Hierarchy of Buying

I SURVEYED MORE than 1,000 business owners to ask "Why do you buy?" See Figure 1.1 for the results.

When the need arises, customers buy first from people they know, trust, and like. The higher on the pyramid you are with your market, the less competition you have. We take it from the top down:

- **Current satisfied customer:** Obviously, people are going to buy from you if they already do and are satisfied. The key term here is "satisfied." Even though customers are current, this doesn't mean they are happy.
- **Referral by a trusted source:** The first thing I do when I need something I don't already have is to ask people I know and trust if they know of a provider, which is easy with sites like Facebook and Twitter. I can get a pile of recommendations in minutes. Are you on the tip of the tongue when someone asks for recommendations within your industry?
- **Current relationship but have yet to purchase:** Potential customers know you, trust you, but have yet to buy from you. And

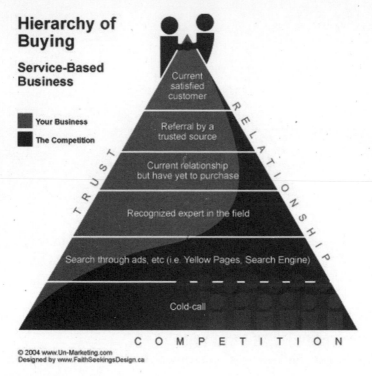

Figure 1.1　Hierarchy of Buying: Service-Based Business

that's okay. The key here is that when they have the need for your product or service, you are in the front of their minds.

- **Recognized expert in the field:** You've built a platform and are consistently in front of potential customers with helpful advice and tips that relate to your industry. You want your market to say, "This guy/girl knows what they're talking about! I need to learn more about them." If done right, this leads them into "current relationship" status.

- **Search through ads, random searches, and so forth:** We get close to the bottom of the barrel here. Potential customers don't know anyone who provides the service, and have never met anyone, so they randomly search for a business that can help. You're not only at the mercy of a search engine here, but price now becomes a huge decider to the point that you almost become a commodity seller. You don't want to be here.

- **Cold call:** Most of your market isn't sitting around saying "You know, I need an accountant to help my growing business, so I'm just going to sit here until someone randomly phones me to offer me that service." Cold-calling is time-intensive with horrible results. Companies encourage it because it has a "low cost" upfront, but what's the cost of annoying 99 people in a row to potentially talk to someone who may hire you based on no trust and price alone? I'm starting a movement to change the phrase from "cold-calling" to "telespam." That will put a stop to the courses; no one is going to sell an ebook about "The Top 10 Ways to Better TeleSpam!"[1]

So the question is simple: Where on the pyramid are you focusing your marketing efforts? The lowest point with high competition and low margins? Or the middle while aiming to get to the top?

The main reason people don't focus on the middle is because it takes time. There, I admitted it. Building trust takes time. Fostering relationships takes time. So if you're looking to make the quick buck, go ahead, slide into the greasy bottom level, and enjoy. Just take a shower afterward.

---

[1] I just jinxed it. Someone is going to write this. I picture a guy with greasy hair who runs multiple free seminars in hotels about how to get rich quick in a time of recession. I go to those events just for the free muffins.

2

A Word on Experts

LET'S THINK BACK to what we learned from the hierarchy of buying. To successfully UnMarket your business, your goal should be to get to the point where you are a recognized expert in your field. You can choose to be recognized for a certain discipline, whether it is time management or sales or marketing in general. You can also aim to be recognized as an expert in a specific industry. What you have to realize is that there is an important difference between somebody who is selling something and somebody who is an expert. This is one of the problems when you use advertising or direct mail for your marketing: If your potential customers do not have an immediate need for your product or service, then you are potentially turning them off and losing them for the future. When you position yourself as an expert with useful information for people, your marketplace will always have a need for that information. You have successfully pulled people into your funnel, you have their attention, and now you need to do something great for them.

Contrary to popular belief, I am not opposed to advertisements or direct mail. It is just that in general these methods are executed poorly. They are almost always doomed to fail, and companies put too much focus on them. Advertising or a listing in the Yellow Pages or (cough) even a cold call can "work" if whoever is in contact with you at that very moment has that exact need. And therein lies the problem. You have to blast your message to tens, if not hundreds of thousands or even millions, of people in a spray pattern just to try to grab a few. When you position yourself as an expert in the field, your message is not only in front of people who want to see it, but they have asked to learn about it.

One of the mistakes I see new business owners make, especially in the service industry, is that they don't consider themselves experts. Countless times I've talked to new clients who balk at the idea of being known as an expert. They tell me they're not ready for that yet. They are adamant that they need to do their work longer to call themselves an expert in their field.

Webster's dictionary defines an *expert* as "having, involving or displaying special skill or knowledge derived from training or experience." You have to be an expert to run your own business. You're not going to be an accountant or a nutritionist or even a virtual assistant if you don't know something about your industry. Sure, you may not be *the* expert in the field, but you can certainly be *an* expert.

People who claim to be the top expert in a certain field often do it in a way that excludes everyone else. In declaring the top spot, these people claim they know the most and everything there is to know about a certain thing. Really, nobody can claim that. Most industries are ever-changing and evolving, as are marketing tools. Of course, customers are always changing, too, as are their needs. A self-proclaimed expert in social media, the one who says that he or she is *the* expert in social media, in a field that didn't exist a year or two ago, should best be avoided.

Pause when you consider hiring someone who calls themselves *the* expert. I understand because I also get uncomfortable sometimes with getting that title of an expert or guru in social media. I am one of the experts in relationship marketing and social media who is a great tool to use for that. But for me to claim that I am *the* expert would be doing a disservice to everybody who is involved in the field.

What is stopping you from calling yourself one of the experts in your field? Being an expert is not an official designation. You don't get a certificate in the mail, nor do you get a cookie. You are an expert when you say you are one. You know how I became an expert in relationship marketing or UnMarketing? I said I was one! This doesn't mean you can become an expert in something you know nothing about. An expert has experience or training in a certain field. Once you have that base set, if you don't have the confidence to call yourself an expert, then you really need to look at yourself. You have to ask, "Why would my customer try to hire me if I don't think I'm great at what I do?"

Once you've accepted the fact that becoming a recognized expert in your field is one of the things you need to do to launch your business off to a great start, we now focus on the term *recognized*. It doesn't do anybody any good to be an expert *only* in your own mind, although this does happen to many people all the time. You don't become an expert by just telling people you're an expert—people tell you and then they tell others. When you are great at what you do, other people will say it for you. So focus on positioning yourself with the knowledge you've obtained and set out to help other people with it unconditionally. Use what I lay out in this book to help put you on the right path to not only positioning yourself but also staying as a recognized expert in your field for a long, long time.

3

Trust Gap

WHY DO YOU buy the things you do? Turn the mirror on yourself for a minute and think about how you make choices about your own purchases.

Trust is one of the main drivers of that hierarchy. The higher the trust, the more likely it is that someone will do business with you. This is an important point in service-based businesses that many business owners fail to recognize. One of the biggest challenges is to get someone to try a service for the first time, so companies offer ways to get you to try it "without risk." Unfortunately, we often equate this with giving something away for free—but this does not always address the issue of trust.

Before speaking at a professional organizers conference, I researched a bunch of their websites and noticed that many organizers were offering a "Free Consultation" of their potential customers' home organizational needs, to get their foot in the door. By focusing only on price as a barrier to making the first purchase, they were missing something important. Of course, I do understand that price objection is a legitimate issue with many potential customers. However, there is also a tremendous trust gap. This is the amount of trust you have to earn before your potential customer will consider buying from you. The trust gap can be practically nonexistent, like buying a newspaper, but even then you have to trust that the content will be good. For many service-based businesses, the trust gap is much wider.

So coming back to the professional organizer example, allowing someone into my home requires a lot of trust, which is not established by simply making it free to try. Then on top of just letting you in, you want me to let you see how horribly unorganized I am? Tack on another huge gap. I'd say right about now, the gap is as big as the Grand Canyon. Focusing on price as the only gap between us is misguided. Taking price away as an issue is like me stepping a foot closer when you're two miles away.

Instead of focusing on the cost, let's look for ways to decrease the gap. As a potential client, I really want to get to know and trust you before I have you in my home and give you access to my mess. If, however, I regularly read great tips on your blog and I get updates via an e-mail newsletter that I signed up for, then I will begin to get to know you.

This is also a great opportunity to look for products you can create that would require less trust and be more scalable.[2] Why not reduce your customers' hesitations and come out with an ebook about *30 Days to a Clutter-Free Home*? Get out to network and meet other people in your industry or local market and let them know about your business. Local businesspeople can become clients and can recommend you to others, which is very valuable.

Just please, for me, don't put the "Free Consultation Offer!" on the back of your business card. It's like going out on a singles night and letting people know you have a "Free Make-Out Offer!"[3]

---

[2] Scalable is the ability to do something in a large amount. An hour of your time isn't scalable, but an ebook is.

[3] Okay, that would be hilarious.

You are not going to this event with the goal of landing a client; you're there to build relationships. We are going to speak often in this book about the difference between your goals and your results. Your goal always needs to be engagement; business will result.

The same goes for a business where your market is made up of solopreneurs—companies that are a one-person show. If, for example, you are a virtual assistant,[4] most likely your website talks somewhere about "freeing up your time." As an entrepreneur running a business alone, no one knows better than I do that I am overworked, and I know I need the help—that's why I am looking on your site. But for me to give away part of my business responsibility is like dropping your kid off at the first day of school. I'm protective and territorial about it and won't just let a person who offers me "One hour free!" to step in and represent my business.

On the other side of that, if you are a solopreneur reading this book, remember that because all points of engagement between your company and your market are potentially UnMarketing opportunities, the people you hire have to be as good as you when they represent it.[5]

Other areas that have a huge trust gap:

- Accounting
- Anything to do with kids
- Wellness practitioners
- Life insurance
- Counseling
- Life coaching

---

[4] It's like having an administrative assistant, but they work from home. I've used them for years. I suggest you do, too.

[5] "Represent" does not have to mean direct client contact. If the client works on research, formatting, or e-mail filtering, it can still affect your brand.

- Lawyers
- Many, many more[6]

Your entire focus when you try to attract new clients in these areas is how you can build trust to reduce that gap. When was the last time a cold call increased trust for you? I thought so.

---

[6] This is the great bullet-point cop-out. When someone writes to me and says, "You forgot this one!" I can just reply, "Ya, that's what I meant by many, many more!"

4

Restaurant That Didn't Get It

WHEN YOU OPEN a new location-based business that relies on a specific geographic clientele, the biggest hurdle you have to overcome is getting people to come to your business the first time. New customer acquisition is where start-up businesses spend most of their marketing dollars. Why not get people to come by using the foundation of human nature—making people feel special?

A friend of mine who runs a graphic design firm brought me in to speak with one of her clients about marketing a new restaurant. She was designing the restaurant's menus and had been asked if she knew anyone who could come up with some unique ways to market the place. I was excited to work with a place that was open to doing things differently. Well, I was wrong about that.[7] But I'm getting ahead of myself.

---

[7] Most business owners who say things like they want to "think outside the box" actually want to do the same things in their box, with better results. It takes courage to do something outside the norm. Most owners like the idea of courage, but few display it in business.

We sat down together for an awesome lunch,[8] and they told me about their vision for the restaurant. They were in a downtown location on the western outskirts of Toronto's core, which is an area with many restaurants. They knew it was going to be a battle to build a customer base.

We discussed a few different things and ideas that they had. We all agreed that their biggest challenge was going to be getting people in the door to try out the food for the first time. The owners had a lot of faith in the quality of their food and service and knew that if we could accomplish getting people to try out the restaurant that they would come back for more.

Perfect! Let's get ready to UnMarket! So here was my proposal:

We need to get a buzz going about the place, but also make people feel exclusive. People love to be made to feel special. Two new condo towers just opened a block away from here, filled with potential customers. I will approach the property management company and let them know that we are going to set aside one night each for the buildings where the residents would have exclusive access to your restaurant.

So far, so good, the owners were smiling.

Here's the kicker. You won't charge them a cent.

Previous smiles were now gone.

You will have two sittings on each night, and people who are interested will have to reserve in advance. When they arrive, they are given your chef's choices of a variety of your best dishes. Not full

---

[8] They gave me the lunch for free. I think I have to say this now due to the new FTC, FCC, NAFTA, and Geneva Convention laws.

meals, but enough collectively so they will be full and content. Since you can seat 40 people at a time, two seatings a night, we will get more than 150 people in here on two weeknights, which wouldn't be busy anyway. These two nights are going to be a great success and get that word of mouth moving.

They just stared at me. I assumed it was because of the shock that set in due to the sheer brilliance they just witnessed. Nope. One replied: "No offense,[9] but that is going to cost us a lot of money! This is a little far-fetched." When I asked them how much it would cost in food, they mentioned maybe a few thousand dollars, which resulted in this exchange:

How much did you guys spend on that magazine ad this month?
About $5,000.
How many customers did it bring in?
We don't know.

It was my turn to stare blankly at them. They weren't biting, so I even offered to guarantee it would work and to withhold any consulting fee until we met an agreed-on attendance rate for those nights. The food cost and my fee would have been less than the amount they paid for that ad, plus the guarantee! No dice.

In the end, they decided not to go with the plan and are no longer in business.[10] Sometimes you've got to think like a customer. Why would I go to your place if I have never heard of it? Trying out your food and service is going to cost me money, and I have to take all the risk. This is amplified in a market where there are tons of competitors, and all kinds of choices that I already trust

---

[9] A surefire way to know you're about to be offended is when someone says this. Also true with "Nothing personal" and "Don't take this the wrong way."

[10] I'm not that cocky to think they went out of business because they didn't use the idea. Just sayin'.

are available. The value of having a packed restaurant would also have affected people walking by, seeing a busy new place filled with people—that is the kind of restaurant they would have come back to try.

If you have confidence in your establishment, your first priority is to get people through that door. They can't come back or tell others about you unless they show up in the first place.

5

Cold Calling

So YOU NEED to remove the trust gap and get people to try you. Now, how exactly are you going to do that? Good question. Almost 10 years ago I was sitting in a friend's office talking about typical guy stuff,[11] when his phone rang. He picked it up, listened for a few seconds, and began to berate the caller on the other end. My favorite line was, "Don't you have anything better to do than to try to sell me your crap?" After he slammed down the phone, we agreed on how big a pain it was when people would cold-call us, interrupting our day. We finished our chat, and then he excused himself with the line, "I gotta go, Scott, I have to make my calls for the day."

I just stared at him with one eyebrow up.

"Chris, you just raked that guy over the coals because he cold-called you, and now you're doing it yourself?"

"No, no, Scott, I'm calling these leads to introduce them to a product they *need!*"

I could already feel the migraine coming on.

---

[11] Nothing of any importance to the world.

And this is where the idea of UnMarketing all began. I had the realization that most companies are guilty of hypocritical marketing. Why do we market to people the way we hate to be marketed to? As business owners or employees, we make sure to hire gatekeepers who don't let pesky salespeople get through, and then we make quotas on how many calls our own representatives have to make.

According to the 2009 Economic Report of the President, 72 percent of Americans signed up for the National Do Not Call List. Two hundred twenty million[12] people collectively said "Stop it!" Yet companies try to get around these loopholes so they can still interrupt our day by trying to pitch their wares.

People still teach courses on how to cold-call better. That's like finding a better way to punch people in the face. People won't like it, but darn it, you can do it better! You hear phrases like, "Every no leads you closer to the next yes!"[13] I know people who become physically ill at the thought of making "their calls." You don't have to do this. If you hate doing something, you will never do it well. In this book we talk about alternatives to cold-calling that are more effective and based on engaging with your market at every point of contact. There is nothing engaging about a cold call.

---

[12] I assume that the people who didn't sign up don't know that they can or are very, very lonely.

[13] I literally had a physical reaction typing that line. I may vomit if I type it again. You've been warned.

6

Aiming Your Company at the Bottom of the Barrel

I REMEMBER THAT 25 years ago I loved leafing through three big books: *Encyclopaedia Britannica*, the *Big Book of Amazing Facts*, and the Yellow Pages. Maybe it was my lack of friends in third grade or avoidance of people commenting on my bulbous head, or just a general interest in things that made me want to go through them. I would sit there for hours.

Fast-forward to the present day. The encyclopedia has been replaced by Wikipedia, the big book is now called the Internet, and the Yellow Pages are called Google. Yet many businesses and phone directory sales reps continue to use these big hunks of paper and try to justify it. I've had this debate with many people about businesses using tools like the Yellow Pages. Most people say it is a great doorstop, booster seat, or a thing to beat people with when they don't pay up on a gambling debt. But let's look at the case that most people say justifies using them, "They work in some markets. People still use them. Like old folks, shut-ins, and people who are still locked into AOL contracts."

So, let's roll with that—people who still potentially use them. I have a few issues with this way of thinking.

- *You are aiming at the bottom of the barrel* (the hierarchy of buying). As you can see when you look at the hierarchy, even people who use the Yellow Pages on occasion will only go to them if they don't already have a service provider, they don't know anybody who could perform the service, they don't know anyone who knows anyone, and they have never even heard of anyone in the field. So no relationships, no word of mouth, nothing. And even if someone got to that point, you would still have to get noticed.

- *Paper spam.* E-mail spam works on the premise that if you blast it out to a million people, a fraction of a fraction may be in the market for the product and a fraction of that may even click. Phone directories work on this same premise. Per year, 1.6 billion pounds of paper are used to produce the 500 million U.S. directories that go in the post. You may be in the market for one of the 2,000 categories of businesses that are listed. It's paper spam at its finest! You didn't opt in, the majority of people don't use it, many do not even take it out of the plastic; instead it ends up in landfill, might get recycled, or thrown at random phone company trucks that drop them off. Sadly, I don't see the books going opt-in, because like most things in the print industry, advertisers are charged based on bloated circulation numbers. And I estimate the number of people who would actually ask for it is 14, give or take 12.[14]

- *Price/competition sensitivity.* The lower down on the hierarchy of buying you are, the most you are up against bargain shoppers and competition. The thing that I have heard the most from former advertisers was that even when they got calls from their

---

[14] If you actually want to opt out, in Canada go to: Delivery.ypg.com/delivery and in the United States: YellowPagesGoesGreen.org

ad, it was usually people looking for the lowest price. This is because you have not built any clout or trust with the potential customers, and you instantly make yourself a commodity. Or even worse, people call who are trying to sell you something, because what better way to sell somebody who advertises in the Yellow Pages than with a cold call.[15] It also becomes a competition of who can have the most "AAAAAA's" in their legal name just to rank as first in their section, or sales reps telling you that you need to buy a bigger ad than your competitor that is right beside you. It fascinates me that businesses pay good money to be listed next to all their local competition.

- *Lack of updates.* Because ads come out from a provider once a year, as soon as your ad is printed, it becomes stale. No testing on which ad converted to leads is better unless you plan on doing it on a year-to-year basis. That would mean to do a proper test using three different ads it would take you years to get any comparable data. It's like walking from Los Angeles to New York to see how your product is doing.

- *A dying market, literally.* Through my totally nonscientific opinion, I am going to guess that the amount of people who use a phone book to look for a service provider goes up with the age demographic. Even senior citizens are ditching them to go online, however. According to PEW Internet and American Life Project, 45 percent of senior citizens over the age of 70 are online, and even 20 percent of those over 76 are surfing the interweb tubes. The average life expectancy is around 80, so I am not sure whom you are aiming for. Those over 80? Go get 'em! Just make sure you buy the big ads with the large fonts.

I understand that there is still a lot of money to be made by businesses that aim for the bottom, when people have exhausted

---

[15] Insert maniacal laughing here with an Alanis Morrisette *Ironic* soundtrack.

every other resource. But even those people are using Google at that point.

The Better Bottom of the Barrel

Considering that Google owns or controls the entire world, I should probably touch on them, but they may be listening, or may even already know what I am about to type.[16] The comparison between the Yellow Pages and Google is so far off that I regret putting them together in the survey. The theory still holds true, which is that you only go searching for something if you don't know the answer already. If I already have a lawyer, I don't go and search Google for another one. But the tools that Google offers for advertisers from click-through tracking to conversion rates to keyword statistics have changed the world of advertising and cannot be compared to the Yellow Pages. So if you must do some kind of advertising, I suggest learning the ins and outs of Google AdWords.[17] Facebook ads have also come on the scene. Same rules apply, with great targeting and demographics.[18]

The flip side to using AdWords is placing them on your site to make some money, which is called *Google AdSense*. It is a simple enough concept: Your site has content and the ads are matched to the content, and when someone clicks on an ad, you get paid from a few cents to a few dollars depending on the topic. This is fine for websites that are purely informational and where there is no person or company attached to it that is trying to position itself as an authority in a marketplace. However, you need to think twice about placing these words on your site or blog. For example, a

---

[16] Excuse me while I go get my tinfoil hat.

[17] If you are looking for some good sites with tips about using Google Adwords, I suggest you Google the term *adwords*.

[18] I found a lawn-care company through Facebook ads, and then they never showed up for the estimate. Ta-da!

copywriter friend of mine decided to place AdWords on her site, which is also where potential clients come to learn about her and to hire her. I asked her why she had the AdWords on the site, and she mentioned that if it made her a little extra money, then what was the harm? I replied that there are multiple things that are hurting her (or you, if you have AdWords on your site).

One concern is that you are sending people away from your site. People leave sites prematurely enough as it is, so you do not need to show them a way out. Is it really worth 6 cents to send someone away from your site? A potential client who is potentially worth hundreds of dollars to you? You can't even do the "open a new window" trick when they click, which would open the site from the ad in another window, leaving your site open. This violates the Google AdWords terms of service.

Another issue is that ads can show competing products, which is good for the competitor and bad for you. Not to mention that you are lending your credibility to whatever that ad is; because the ad is on your site, it is almost an endorsement. The ads are blended so well that they almost look like they are a part of your site. This makes it look pretty but can play with the customer's perception.

If you are aiming for the bottom of the hierarchy of buying, then Google AdWords is a great tool, but I would rather aim higher.

7

Pull and Stay

AFTER THE COLD-CALLING episode, the other event that pushed me over the edge into the UnMarketing world was an event called *Art by the Lake* in my hometown. Artists gather down by our shoreline and set up in tents, displaying their paintings, sculptures, and photographs. It's well attended and looks like a great success, but I noticed a problem.

The problem was not with the attendees. They were great—enjoying themselves walking into each artist's tent, admiring the work, making comments, and giving compliments. The artists, unfortunately, were not nearly as engaging. Most were sitting in lawn chairs, halfheartedly thanking people for their kindness, but you could just tell they were secretly saying to themselves, "If you like it, why don't you buy it?!?"

The ratio of lookers to buyers was at least 100 to 1. The artists were doing the old-school method of sales, which I like to call "push-and-pray marketing." Push something out there and pray people buy it. People are there to look at all these great art pieces; they were even saying to the artists that they might be interested in buying from them eventually. The most I saw any of the artists do was to hand them a card and say "Let me know!" and then, nothing. With that, the crowd of potential customers would move on to the next tent.

What were the artists hoping these people were going to do? Go home, realize they had a perfect spot in their living room for one of their paintings or sculptures, and try to remember who the artist was? Here every vendor had a prime opportunity for engagement. Crowds of people were raising their hands expressing interest in the artists' products, but they were just being allowed to walk away.

Let's take the artists' situation and use the pull-and-stay method instead. You pull customer information and stay in front of them. Let's imagine that you are one of the artists at Art in the Park. Someone comes into your tent and mentions how wonderful the work is, especially your landscape photography. Instead of just saying thanks, you could say, "I appreciate it. I regularly take landscapes, and it's amazing how well they're received. I know it's tough to decide on art, especially when there are so many great artists here today. I have an exclusive preview e-mail I send out to people when I take new shots. I could also send you some shots of what is here today. Would you like to sign up? No charge." Now you control the contact. After potential customers visit 50 other booths this day at the show, they will remember that you are the only one who stood out after the event is long over. Now you can start to build the relationship.

Take it another step. That night, after taking the visitors' e-mail addresses, write to them to say thank you for coming by the booth. Send them a few shots and ask what they thought about the event. Start a conversation. Engage with them, get to know your marketplace. You'll be amazed at the responses you receive.

We talk much more about how to pull and stay potential customers at shows like this when we talk about trade shows later on.

The same methods can also be applied to retail. Remember, marketing is not one department of your business; it is every point of engagement, including sales. The mistake made by too many businesspeople is that if shoppers do not want to buy immediately, they just let them walk away when they should be UnMarketing and pulling in these potential customers.

8

Reasons Why Companies Don't Use Social Media

NO MATTER HOW many times I sing the praises of social media, no matter how many case studies I present, company reps always give me an excuse of why they can't jump in. They say they have no time, there is no ROI (return on investment), they have no control, or there is no geographic boundary if they are local.

If you say you have no time to listen and to talk with people in your marketplace, then you are saying that you have no time for your customers. You need to make time to be in that conversation. If you believe business is built on relationships, then what could possibly be more important?

Return on investment (ROI) is one of the lamest excuses that I hear all the time. Most old-school salespeople could never calculate their efforts in ROI in the first place. I ask them what their ROI is on the networking event that they drove to last week or the conference that they just attended to see their current customers. It is more ROR (return on relationships) and, truthfully, that is really hard to calculate.

25

A classic move is to want to control the message. Company reps are used to having to go through multiple layers and approvals before being released to the public via a news chain. The funny thing is that they never had control even before social media. It is just that now people have a voice that can be heard.

Local businesspeople say that social media is fine for someone like me who has borderless clientele but no good for them because they only serve a limited geographic area. As you see in the next few sections, social media can actually be better for local-based businesses than for anyone else.

9

Social Media (Social Currency as Well)

THE PROBLEM WITH the term *social media* is that whenever people see the word "media" they automatically think "push." Media has been classically linked as a way to push your message out through a variety of methods such as television, newspapers, radio, and online.

However, social media isn't media at all—it is simply a conversation with two or more people. It's an action. Not a site. Social media isn't Twitter. Or Facebook. It isn't the new website flavor of the week. It's the ability to have conversations online with others, whether it is your market, customers, colleagues, or anyone who happens to come across your conversation.

Twitter isn't social media if you use it to just send out ads and blog post updates. That's a glorified RSS feed in 140 characters. You have people every day talking about your market, your industry, and possibly your actual product or service. You choose whether to be part of it, but that won't stop the conversation, and sometimes will make it worse if people view you as ignoring an issue. Out of the top 100 brands mentioned on Twitter, the majority don't have an official account.[19] Imagine a room of a thousand

---

[19] Via BrandRepublic http://bit.ly/cY1f8A

of your potential and current customers all talking about you and you choose to go somewhere else. Or even worse, you show up to the party and just hand out flyers, which is what you're doing if you run a Twitter account and only send out ads. The existence of the account makes it look like you want to be part of the conversation, but your actions show otherwise.

Facebook isn't social media if you just run a fan page and then don't interact with the people who join it. Facebook is a 2.0 mailing list, and an ineffective one at that. Sure, sending out a request for someone to "Be our fan!" on Facebook so they can be informed of discounts could grab you some people and may create a few sales, too, if you're a known brand to them, but think of how much more you could benefit if you engaged with those new fans. What would that do to your reputation? People want to be validated, they want to be heard, and they want to feel they matter. You shouldn't have to ask someone to be a fan—if you engage people, they become fans. Raging ones.

LinkedIn isn't social media if all you're doing is hunting down potential customers and trying to pitch to them through five different gatekeepers and asking, "Hey Scott, can you forward this on to your friend you've built trust with? I got a whopper of a deal!" The site has so much potential and yet is used properly so rarely. For an example of this, check out most of the LinkedIn Groups. They are full of push articles from people reposting the same thing, which are mostly sales pitches. No conversation, no comments, just crap. Start topics of conversations, help people out.

Writing a blog isn't using social media unless you are social with your readers. A blog without the ability to comment by the readers is just an informal article that may as well stay in print. If you're not open to conversation, why be in a channel where people expect it? You potentially do more harm than good by being there and not engaging than you would by not being there at all.

Company reps are scared to use social media in this manner, though, because they've always had the misconception that they can control the message—the press release, the well-spun message approved by three departments. They have to realize something very quickly: They *never* controlled the message, because it's in the receiver's hands to absorb, experience, and spread their own experience with your message in their eyes. You may have a well-crafted press release about your new baby stroller, but moms will give you their own spin, which has no spin at all. They share the good, the bad, and the ugly.[20]

If you want to be successful in social media, you have to build up your social currency. Whenever I try to explain social media to a person or audience, I tend to get that dazed puppy look staring back at me. So I now relate it to money. Think of it this way: You wouldn't open a business bank account and ask to withdraw $5,000 before depositing anything. The banker would think you are a loony. Yet people go on social media, open their account, send out a few pitches for their mediocre ebook, and then complain to me that this social media stuff "doesn't work."

You've got to invest in something before withdrawing. Investing your social currency means giving your time, your knowledge, and your efforts to that channel before trying to withdraw monetary currency. I tweeted 10,000 times before ever trying to pitch something on Twitter. But when I did, I sold it out in a day (UnBootcamp).[21] People don't care about your business until they know you care about them. Look what gets shared on Facebook or retweeted on Twitter. It's not ads or pitches. It's knowledge. It's stuff that makes people say "awesome," and they need to tell others about it.

---

[20] In word of mouth, there are two groups you never want to anger: moms and religious people. And if you annoy religious moms? Well, let's just say you better brush up on your praying skills.

[21] Picture this: five weeks of my ranting to help your business. www.Un-Bootcamp.com

10

Twitter versus Facebook versus LinkedIn versus Google+

So I'VE CONVINCED you to give it a try. The problem—or the great thing, depending on how you look at it—is that there are many options for where and how to start building your social currency.

How do you choose where to start? The main players in social networking for business are currently Facebook, Twitter, LinkedIn, and Google+. They all have their pros and cons and can all be beneficial for your business, depending on your market and needs. Here is a little bit of information about each one.

Facebook

Facebook is the biggest of the three social media sites we are going to discuss. It was originally started as a U.S. college-based networking site and now has more than a trillion active users,[22] with 70 percent of them being outside of the United States.

---

[22] Actual Facebook stats from www.Facebook.com/press/info.php?statistics. A trillion is an estimate to keep the book relevant in 2050.

Common Terms

Friend: The name for the people you connected with.

Wall: The hub of your activity, where people can read, post, and comment.

Tag: Connecting pictures, articles, and videos to specific friends who appear.

Poke: A virtual poke in the shoulder to say hi. Never, ever do this to people. It's not only awkward, but I am not sure that "poking" people is something you want to associate with your brand.

Like: The virtual thumbs-up to anything from your friend's or business's status on Facebook to a blog post off Facebook. Millions of sites have adopted the button. If you click it on their site, it adds the link to your Facebook profile, recommending it to your friends.

The Good

Facebook not only has a high number of users, but more than half of them log in every day.

The ability to create fan/business pages and groups allows companies to have a hub within a community that is already established.

One of the great things about the newest version of Facebook[23] is that it rewards you for engagement with your followers. This is called *presumed relevancy*,[24] where

---

[23] And by newest I mean, now its old since you are reading this book in print and it is probably as relevant as talking about the new update for the Commodore 64.

[24] Thanks to Jay Baer, the author of www.ConvinceandConvert.com, for the term that I wish I had thought of.

Facebook chooses what appears in your stream based on what you and your friends have commented on and/or liked. So the goal on Facebook is no longer just quantity of fans for your page, but frequent, relevant posts and updates that engage those fans.

The Bad

You have to get approval to connect with someone by adding that person as a friend. On Facebook, when you want to connect with someone, you send that person a friend request. Before you can engage with the friend, the person has to accept that request. Vice versa, you will get requests from other people and decide if you want to be their friend. I do not like that you need to get someone's permission to learn from them.

Apps and notifications (e.g., Farmville, MafiaWars invites) can get really annoying to many people. We talk more about some of these apps in the next section of the book when we discuss social media sins.[25]

LinkedIn

LinkedIn is a strictly professional networking website. It has more than 100 million users as of 2011. Wikipedia describes the purpose of the site:

> . . . to allow registered users to maintain a list of contact details of people they know and trust in business.

---

[25] It got so bad on Facebook that I got inspired to sing a song (WhyDontYouLeaveMeAlone.com).

Common Terms

Connections: The people on the list are called *Connections*. Users can invite anyone (whether a site user or not) to become a connection.

Recommendations: The ability to give testimonials for specific job roles on your profile from others.

The Good

With only business users, the focus is more tightly on business networking.

Gives a great amount of business information for each person.

The Bad

Sending a request to contact someone must go through potentially multiple gatekeepers.

Groups have great potential, but they are mostly full of self-serving articles and sales pitches.

Twitter

There are 200 million using only 140 characters at a time.[26]

Common Terms

Tweet: The name of the message you send out, 140 characters or less.

Follower: A person who has chosen to read your tweets on an ongoing basis.

(continued)

---

[26] http://Mashable.com/2011/07/16/twitter-accounts-200-million/

(*continued*)

Retweet: The act of repeating what someone else has tweeted so that your followers can see it.

Hashtag: Start with the symbol "#". It is a theme for the tweet that allows all similar tweets to be searched.

The Good

Immediate conversations and connections.

No apps or groups, just conversation.

No barrier to engage in relationships.

The Bad

A tweet has very little shelf-life.

High dropout of new users. It can take a little bit for users to get Twitter, and often they stop using the site before they figure out how it works.

It's the "no barrier" to communication from Twitter that really sold me. Because both LinkedIn and Facebook are permission-first sites, I need to "know" you before getting to know you, which makes no sense when you're trying to meet other business owners. I use Facebook and LinkedIn as secondary levels. Once I've gotten to know someone on Twitter, we can go to the next level on either of those two sites because I now "know" them.

Google+

Google's entry into the social media pants party, which was launched to much fanfare in early 2011.

Common Terms:

+1: The equivalent to Facebook's like button. The term is a popular internet meme, meaning "I approve."

Circles: Circles are choosing whose content you read and who can see yours. Commonly misunderstood, the other person has to add you to their circle for you to see their posts. It's like showing up to the pants party with a hula-hoop. You can say who you want in the hoop, but they have to choose to get in.

Hangouts: I'd call this a private pants party, but since it's video based, you should probably bring your entire wardrobe to it. Limited to a small number of participants, it's a cool way to video chat in a group setting. I've done a few hangouts with close circles of mine. I wouldn't open it up to the public. To see why, Google "chat roulette."

Posts: Function a lot like Facebook's wall. People can comment, +1, and share your posts.

The Good and the Bad

Google+ functions much better out of the gate than any of the other networks, but that is partially because it has the benefit of learning from the others' screw-ups. Its like the dude who shows up with the brand-new version of a car you got three years ago. Of course it's going to be better, and it kind of makes him look like a prick.

Google+ isn't a "Facebook killer," it simply is what it is, another social network that I talk to the same people on. The circle aspect is genius, but I also think it is misunderstood and could be the main hindrance to mass adoption of the network. But, since your mom isn't on there yet, you still feel kind of cool using it—and that alone makes it worth trying out.

11

Social Media Platforming

THERE ARE TOO many choices when it comes to social media. You've got the networking-style sites (Twitter, Facebook, LinkedIn), blogs (yours and others), social bookmarking (Digg, Reddit, Delicious), and video sharing (YouTube). No one can possibly use all of them all the time and create any sort of presence, which is why you need to build a social media platform.

A decade ago,[27] I used to manage bands in Toronto, and it was always said, "Before you can fill a stadium, you have to fill a club." So even though your dream is to play in front of thousands, try filling a club with a hundred first. Same goes for social media. Most people want the million views on YouTube, 100,000 followers on Twitter, and to be hitting the front page of Digg every week, but that's not going to happen right away, and it will never happen if you try to do it all at once.

Build a small stage—your platform—that you're going to stand on and get people to come to. Pick one place where you want people to find you and play your best "show" there for as long as it

---

[27] You know you are old when you start talking about your work experience in decades.

takes to build a solid following. If you tell people to come find you on Twitter, become a fan on Facebook, read your blog, and watch your videos on YouTube when you first encounter them, they're going to run the other way.

There are three steps to successfully building your platform: (1) traction, (2) momentum, and (3) expansion. You have to start by building traction. Social media can be a very challenging tool to use when you are just starting out. You post a few comments, send out a tweet or two, post your blog, and no one answers. It is easy to write it off as not working. Even if you have followers, only a small percentage of your followers are online or will see any given tweet or post, and a fraction of those will reply to you. The best advice I have is to jump in. On Twitter especially, there is no such thing as interruption. The biggest regret of people who have gained traction is that they wish they had jumped in sooner.

When you are building traction, consistency is very important. If you have a few hours per week to commit to social media, that time is more effective if you spread it out rather than spending it all in one big chunk every week. Find people you want to follow; learn from and get to know them and then start replying to them, or sharing things they have said. Think of things that you can tweet or post that are helpful to others and engaging. Ask questions and be there to discuss the answers.

Once you have gained traction, you are now in the second phase of platforming—momentum. Now remember that this can happen at different points for different people and businesses. How you define your goals for social media is up to you. If you have reached a point where you are getting something out of the network, then you are here. This is not about a number of followers or fans, it is about engagement. This is not the time for you to get lazy. Momentum is the time when you switch from looking for new relationships toward enhancing current ones. Sites like Twitter are great for initially getting to know someone, but if you really want to enhance relationships, it's time to take them to the next level. This is where social media and the real world start to mix. Going anywhere from a local tweetup[28] to a major conference in your industry, social media can be an incredible tool for before, during, and after the event.

Momentum is also the stage where you are going to want to manage your social media use more efficiency. Using a desktop application such as TweetDeck or Hootsuite sorts your activity into columns and allows you to manage your activity on multiple sites, and applications like UberTwitter for your smartphone allow you to keep up while on the go. The last thing you want to do is to start getting momentum somewhere and become overwhelmed and end up leaving. Don't be fooled by social media gurus who tell you that social media is a great way to build relationships without effort. Nothing out there will ever change the fact that relationships take time.

You have to be wary of expectations. Servicing requests/concerns of your market when you only have a few talking to you is easy, but it can quickly get out of hand if you do not manage expectations. Answering a tweet about your product at 2 AM makes you look like you are dedicated but soon turns into an expectation. One company doing a great job of this across all platforms is VistaPrint. I was especially impressed with how they manage expectations on their Twitter account.[29] On their main page, within their bio they mention the hours that they are available to answer tweets. They start the day with a good morning sign-in and end with a goodbye sign-off, including the customer service toll-free number in case an important issue comes up outside of these hours. When I asked Jeff Esposito, the PR Manager for VistaPrint,

---

[28] A tweetup is a casual get-together of Twitter friends where you are allowed to speak in more than 140 characters. Imagine that?

[29] Twitter.com/Vistaprint

about the way they manage follower expectations, he said, "The last thing we wanted to do was to make it look like we weren't listening. Since we have customers around the world, we wanted to make sure they knew they mattered. The worst thing you can do is to show people you are listening to some and not others."

The third stage of platforming is expansion. For me, launching my blog marked this point. I purposefully grew my platform on Twitter first and waited until I knew I could drive readers and commenters to the site. It is one thing to send a tweet or even a post on Facebook and have no replies, but to write a 500- to 800-word blog post and have no one read it is really hard. It is also important to expand your platform to take your dialogue with followers to the next level and grow the relationship. I started mine after someone asked me what I would do if Twitter went down unexpectedly one day.[30]

Now just because you have written a post and uploaded it, you can't just starting wearing your "I'm web 2.0" T-shirt. A blog without the ability to engage is just called an *article*. It is the ability to interact within the comment system that changes a post from being static to ecstatic. There are a variety of free tools to allow threaded comments.[31] The one I am currently using, Disqus,[32] not only allows threaded comments but also sends me a notification and reply to a comment directly through e-mail. This way I can keep up on comments and reply to relevant ones that turn into conversations that enhance the quality of the post. I can also reply with the word *delete* and it will instantly remove the comment from the blog if it is spam or hateful in any way. It's crucial that commentators are notified of a reply via e-mail (if they choose),

---

[30] If and when this happens, I will be the guy curled up in the fetal position in the corner, sobbing. Please give generously.

[31] Threaded means you allow people to reply underneath the original comment, like a message board that creates conversation.

[32] www.Disqus.com

otherwise they won't know you have replied to them and the conversation stops.

I choose not to moderate comments, meaning that I do not approve before they are posted. I find moderation of this kind stifles momentum and conversation because of the delay. You lose the initial emotion moment that led to the comment in the first place, making it less likely for people to pass around the blog on which they have commented.

You need to be wary about building your entire "empire" on somebody else's site. I love it when people on Facebook form protest groups about a new change on the site, when it is neither their site nor do they pay anything to use it.[33] You are also fighting through a million other voices on those sites. For example, when I started my big push on Twitter, it hadn't yet hit the mainstream.[34] It was much easier for any single tweet of mine to get noticed because I wasn't competing with a million other marketers, Ashton Kutcher, or somebody's cat.

One of the dangers of trying to expand too early to multiple platforms is that you are tempted to promote them all to everyone at once. I get direct messages from people on Twitter constantly, before I know much about them, telling me to come add them on Facebook or LinkedIn. No, no, let's get to know each other within the platform we met on first.[35]

It also makes sense to match your platform with your market. Playing heavy metal in a jazz club isn't going to work so well, so whatever your platform location is, make sure your audience is

---

[33] It's like me inviting you over for dinner and you complaining about the plastic on my couch. I only take that off for special company.

[34] *Mainstream* meaning Oprah talked about it.

[35] Asking me to join you on another social networking site when we just met on a different one is like meeting me at a networking event and immediately asking me to go to a different one. I haven't even figured out if you're creepy yet or not, let alone becoming a networking chum.

ready for it. If you want them to subscribe to your blog, and the audience isn't tech geeks, you better make sure you offer more than an RSS feed to subscribe. Years ago I had a conversation with an online video producer, before the days when high-speed connections were the norm. He ranted about how online video was grainy and he wouldn't reduce the quality of videos just to save bandwidth. I wished him well and told him to enjoy his videos, because he'd be the only one watching them. Today it's a different story, his market has adopted higher bandwidth, and high-quality streaming video is the norm. He was just a few years early for his show to start. ☺

12

HARO — Platforming Example

NO ONE ILLUSTRATES the social media platforming concept better than Peter Shankman, who runs the very popular newsletter *Help a Reporter Out* (HARO).

While running the Geek Factory, Inc., Peter wanted to find a way to connect journalists with sources outside of his client roster. He picked Facebook as his initial platform and created a group called *Help a Reporter Out* where he would send out requests he received from journalists for sources about a variety of topics. This wasn't anything new, because there were a few services out there that did it. The difference was that he was doing it for no charge. Knowing what could happen if he built up the platform, he wanted to build a wild community of fans and subscribers. It soon outgrew the Facebook group setting, and he turned it into a newsletter style at www.HelpAReporter.com. Three times a day (morning, afternoon, and evening) he sends out a listing of journalist requests for experts on every topic in the world, it seems.

With more than 100,000 sources subscribed (including myself), Peter has built a huge supportive list. He protects the integrity of

42

the list like a rabid wolf, letting it be known that if anyone misuses the requests for information by spamming reporters, he will not only remove them, he will out them to the list. I remember the first time I read this, I actually said, "Yeah!" When was the last time something you wrote in your newsletter made a reader yell "Yeah!"?[36]

Such a strong list, with rumors that it gets a 90 percent open rate, is in another stratosphere than most newsletter publishers will ever achieve. Peter sells one ad per edition, but the key here is that the ads are written by him, with his comments. It almost makes them feel like they aren't an ad. They make me smile or, at the very least, curious, so I want to learn more about the product or service, and I click to take a look. At just more than $1,000 per ad cost, three issues a day, he pulls in more than $1 million a year from these ads alone, with placements being sold out months in advance. Not bad for starting out as a Facebook group.

Peter does two things really well: he builds a list of rabid fans and he engages with them (he is active with them on Twitter, Facebook, and answers e-mail). He inserts personality into what he does, so it's worth its weight in gold.

---

[36] Shoot me an e-mail at Yeah@Un-Marketing.com if anything in this book makes you say "Yeah!" out loud, too. Bonus points if you say "Yeah!" and it wakes a person or animal up in your house.

13

The Game Has Changed

Immediacy and Relevancy

ALONG WITH THE explosion of social media comes a change in power. One person calling your customer service line to complain may not have much impact in your mind, but throw in a handful of people with the same problem, an influential blog or two, and a Twitter army, and you have a good old-fashioned revolt on your hands.

Nothing defines this more than when Motrin decided to launch a new ad campaign around "Motrin Moms." It was a little edgy, a bit shortsighted, and missed the mark. The ad was trying to say that carrying a baby in one of those side-saddle-shoulder harnesses was done because it looks trendy, but because it also hurts, you should take Motrin!

The company released the spot on its website on a Friday in late 2008. I'm sure the company reps gave a round of high-fives to each other,[37] and off they went for the weekend—and then the

---

[37] I'm sure the creative team did not include many moms, just a bunch of people who thought they knew what a mom is like.

baby-poo hit the fan. Moms who watched the commercial got offended[38] and started to talk about it on blogs, on Facebook, and on this up-and-coming micro-blogging site named Twitter. I would not have wanted to be the guy who showed up at the office Monday morning to the 20,000 e-mails that were awaiting Motrin in response to its new campaign.

Here was a billion-dollar pharmaceutical company versus a bunch of moms. In the old days, big pharma wins. Company reps send a few coupons in the mail to irate callers, and that's the end of it. But now, everything is immediate and everyone's voice is relevant. Social media is the great level playing field for all. Blogs and tweets rank very well in search engines, and word of mouth is as easy to start as a single tweet. Go ahead and search Google for the term *Motrin Moms*. See what comes up. The results are dominated by blog posts about how bad the commercial is, or a rundown of how badly it was handled by Motrin reps. The Motrin reps do not even own the top-five ranking for the term![39]

They pulled the commercial off the corporate site, but it was too late. YouTube has at least 10 copies of it more than a year later. Remember, the Internet never forgets. ☺

So what could Motrin execs have done to fix this situation, outside of never creating the commercial in the first place? Here are five suggestions:

1. Monitored social media channels for mentions of the advertisement or campaign. If people are talking about your brand, you should be a part of the conversation.
2. Reacted and posted in their blog, in place of the commercial, that they were attempting to have some fun and admitted to the error.

---

[38] Some say too offended, which is always smart to do. Tell someone they're overreacting. That goes over well.

[39] At this writing in 2011, the actual corporate Motrin site ranked thirteenth.

3. Run a contest to have others make a better commercial about Motrin Moms and given away prizes, such as those baby slings, and so forth.
4. Enabled voting on Facebook, via tweets, and on YouTube for the best commercial.
5. Presented the commercial as what they should have done in the first place because the people who know moms best are . . . moms.

We are a very forgiving culture if you own up to your mistakes. You can't avoid mistakes, nor can you control them after the fact, but you can own a mistake and make it better. When someone says "Any publicity is good publicity," that's true to a point. If you remedy the situation, it can turn out great for you, but if you don't fix it, it just makes you look bad, and I can't see how that's good publicity for anyone.

14

Publicized Customer Service

COMPANIES ARE ACCUSTOMED to one-on-one customer service. Call centers, e-mails, and help desks are all based on the idea that you need one employee interaction for every customer reaction. What social media allows is for businesses to have these interactions in public. This kind of public customer service can be both good and bad for your brand. Good, because it allows people to see that you are listening and engaging and care about customer service. Other customers who share these concerns or questions may potentially solve their own issue without having to ask you individually after seeing the interaction online. The bad can happen if the business account is run by someone who is not skilled at customer service or when complaints are ignored.

A great example of the benefit of public customer service comes from Tufts University in Massachusetts. They have three cafeterias, all with Twitter accounts. Their primary function is tweeting out their daily menu for students to see, and more importantly listening to what students are saying about them—as the following tweets show:

humblebeauty: I've just eaten the most DISGUSTING apple in the world. How do you grow something so horrible tasting? get it together! **@tuftsdining**.

1 day ago from *web* · Reply · View Tweet

As you can see, she is using Twitter like a lot of people do, to vent. This is usually where many companies do nothing and either the tweet dies (yet always lives on Google) or she gets even angrier. Smart organizations pick up on this and realize they have a chance to not only solve an issue, but to build a reputation.

TuftsDining: **@humblebeauty** Sorry about the apple. Which location did you get it from?

about 14 hours ago from *HootSuite* · Reply · View Tweet · Show Conversation

Within a few hours, the cafeteria mentioned responded with the above tweet. As you can see, they showed that they were listening, that they cared, and that they wanted to do something about it. What happened next is very important to see:

humblebeauty: **@TuftsDining** It's ok. I've just never had one that was so bad before. I got it from Dewick.

about 13 hours ago from *web* · Reply · View Tweet · Show Conversation

Notice from her first two words, "It's ok," that she is already backing off, and the situation has potentially been diffused because of the cafeteria's acknowledgment. It could have been left at that, but they decided to ensure her experience would be as good as it could be after this mistake.

TuftsDining: **@humblebeauty** Thanks for the location info. Yes, it's fresh fruit and sometimes they go bad, but we should catch it before it gets to you

about 4 hours ago from *HootSuite* · Reply · View Tweet · Show Conversation

Here they again acknowledge her and own the mistake. They could have gone another route and just said, "Fresh fruit goes bad, that's life," but they didn't.

In general, people are understanding and forgiving if a company simply acknowledges them and owns their error. They didn't even have to offer her another apple or fruit; just the fact that they listened and engaged with her makes them already stand out above the rest. If this same dialogue occurred over the phone or e-mail, the customer service ends at one person. This way, it allows exponentially more people to experience the one act of customer service.

So if we have to talk about ROI in social media, what would it be worth to you to have to take less customer service calls, have fewer people talking negatively about you, and get more people seeing that your company cares about its customers?

As I told you, things do not always go this well. With the wrong person managing your social media account, one negative customer service experience may also exponentially grow. A perfect example of this is the experience April Dunford had when she complained about one of her local coffee shops, Dark Horse Café.

You run a cafe. About 50% of your customers are working on laptops. You have one electrical outlet. I'm talking about you Mr. Dark Horse.

10:44 AM Jan 15th from Tweetie   ↩ Reply ♡ ↑

aprildunford
April Dunford

April is doing something that many Twitter users do: Posting a concern about service she is getting at an establishment. She does not direct the concern at the Dark Horse account, simply rants a little about wanting more outlets.

Hey @darkhorsecafe, check it out:
http://twitter.com/aprildunford
/statuses/7791578235 (via
@aprildunford)

10:46 AM Jan 15th from TweetDeck

jkozuch
Justin Kozuch

One of April's followers on Twitter sees the complaint and directs it at the Dark Horse accounts, stirring the customer service pot. A few hours later, Dark Horse sees the complaint and replies. Remember how well the Tufts University cafeteria handled their critic . . .

@aprildunford that's awesome... we are in the coffee business, not the office business. We have plenty of outlets to do what we need...

4:09 PM Jan 15th from web in reply to aprildunford   ↶ Reply ↻ R

darkhorsecafe
Dark Horse Espresso

As you can see, there is no acknowledgment by the café that they have done anything wrong. They do not demonstrate understanding at all. You should know that many of their customers are entrepreneurs who do work while they enjoy their coffee and food, so needing an outlet would likely have been a common customer concern. They do not leave it here, deciding to send April one more tweet to make sure she understands how unimportant her issue is to them.

@aprildunford maybe you should just
enjoy the cafe and take a break from you
computer for a few minutes... enjoy the
space you are in.

4:12 PM Jan 15th from web in reply to aprildunford   ← Reply ⟲ Retv

darkhorsecafe
Dark Horse Espresso

I am pretty sure this reaction is the worst possible thing that
the Dark Horse could have done. They had a huge opportunity
here, a point of contact with a customer in public. They could
have ignored her, which would have been significantly better than
this. They could have simply said they heard her, understood there
was a problem, and appreciated her feedback. They could have
taken the point, perhaps used Twitter to ask some of their other
customers if they shared the concern, and improved their service.

Here is April's reply, which by the way is considerably kinder
than mine would have been:

@darkhorsecafe Sorry I mentioned it.
Sometimes I show people stuff on my
computer (over coffee). Please ignore
the cust. feedback.(gee whiz)

5:18 PM Jan 15th from Uber Twitter in reply to darkhorsecafe   ← Reply ⟲

aprildunford
April Dunford

You know the next time I am going to go to the Dark Horse
Café? Never! This message reached a lot of people, not only April's
followers, but through retweets as well. You need to take advantage
of the potential for great public customer service that social media
can allow, but you also need to know what can go wrong. Another
potential of public service happens when you watch your competitors' interactions online. If I owned a café near the Dark Horse, I

would have had an outlet with April's name on it, taken a picture, and tweeted it out to her with an invitation for a coffee on-the-house. People are online right now talking about you and your competition. Are you listening?

To pick a fight, or say hello to April, go to www.Rocket Watcher.com.

15

Don't Bank on the Bold

THE OLD SAYING is that the squeaky wheel gets the oil, and online it is no different. The angry bloggers, tweeters, and posters who shout the loudest get the most attention. We give a lot of consideration to the people who are bold, who phone us, write to us, and protest, yet they are always a very small representation (1 percent) of our total marketplace. Most people will not say anything directly to you at all, and these are the ones you should be listening to. As you focus on calming the angry few, many more of your customers may be mildly dissatisfied or just tolerating your level of service or the quality of your product. They have not yet been pushed far enough for you to lose their business, but they are in a vulnerable state where your competitors can easily win them over. People are not confrontational by nature; they will speak only by taking their money elsewhere, and they won't even say goodbye, they will just go. Sites like Twitter and Facebook allow customers to vent about dissatisfaction in a casual environment, allowing you access to your less-bold customers.

The same holds true on the other side of the spectrum. You may hear the occasional shout-out or comment from a bold happy customer, which is always wonderful for any business to hear. However, the vast majority of your happy customers will go on using your product quietly. Social media allows these more moderate praises to reach your business regularly, along with suggestions for ways to improve your product or service.

The thing that gets me really riled up about people questioning the ROI of social media is: If I offered you a tool 10 years ago that allowed you to listen and respond to the casual conversations of your potential, current, and past customers, you would have paid me $20,000 a month for this eighth wonder of the world. But now that it is here, and it's free, you question its value? This is why I get ulcers. It's like extremely smart businesspeople become temporarily dumb; it baffles my mind.

16

Seven Deadly Social Media Sins

SOCIAL MEDIA IS so new that most people are making it up as they go,[40] but most people seem to make the same mistakes—or, dare I say, sins. We look at the biggest players online for business—Facebook, Twitter, and LinkedIn—but the same concepts can be applied to any social media site.

Greed

Greed is quite a popular sin. Twitter is a self-centered tool. It's about us. But it's 100 times better if used as a conversational tool versus a dictation. I see people using Twitter as a glorified RSS feed for their blog or an ad-puker. So absent of personality, I wonder why they even try. Yes, they are in business, but if they believe that business is built on relationships, they need to make building them their business.

---

[40] Nothing proves this more than the increase of social media experts from 5,000 in May 2009 to almost 16,000 listed on Twitter in December 2009. As of Fall 2011, they've all moved on to being QR code experts. (source: WhatsNextBlog.com).

This sin holds a special place for the people who only retweet compliments about themselves. I was talking to a colleague of mine, and she was asking how I have built such a large amount of followers. I mentioned that I get retweeted a lot and I retweet others. Her reply was "I retweet others all the time!" When I checked out her page, the only time she *ever* retweeted anyone was if it was a compliment about her or a #FollowFriday[41] mention with her in it. You may as well tweet while looking in a mirror telling yourself you're good enough, you're smart enough, and gosh darn it, people like you.

Facebook is in a world of its own. People do everything from posting on someone's wall with a seven-line signature, to mass-inviting people to every event (even if the event is local and the person is not even in the same country), to tagging people in articles that they are not even mentioned in just to get them to read it. There is a special vein in my forehead that you can clearly see when these things occur. Someone didn't become your friend on Facebook to give you business or to allow you to use his or her wall as a billboard. Even the term *friend* means a relationship, and you are not building one when you invite me to your Multi-Level Marketing (MLM) event in San Diego and I live in Toronto. Instead, use Facebook to engage and to comment on people's posts and status updates and to share links with them that they may like, not ones you have written to promote yourself but ones you have found that may help them.

LinkedIn falls under the same issues that Facebook does. The group's function has so much great potential because the site is fully business-oriented, yet the majority of the groups and posts that I have seen during my research were either outright spam or drive-by articles. Drive-by articles are those that are posted in multiple groups and sites, which are mostly a thinly veiled pitch

---

[41] #FollowFriday is a tradition on Twitter where you suggest people to others to follow.

for the author's services. Some gurus also teach this method, but you will notice that the original authors are never around when someone has a follow-up question. I hope that the LinkedIn discussion groups become just that, groups that have great discussion.

Gluttony

Get followers fast!!!! Most people on Twitter have seen tweets like this or thought of using a site that helps kick-start things for you. Seems innocent, right? Let's just have a look-see at this logic. Imagine a guy just followed you. Makes you feel all warm and fuzzy that a new person is along for the Twitter journey with you, makes up for your lack of popularity in high school, and the day is getting better. Then you go to his profile and you see a bunch of tweets that say:

> I have found a way to get thousands of followers fast and auto-mated!! Go to this site!

How does that make you feel now? Still warm and fuzzy? Still getting tingles? Didn't think so. When you tweet out "follower system" tweets, it says one thing: You're in it for the numbers. I'll bet the 3 cents I still have after my latest trip to Vegas that one of the next tweets will be about an "amazing business." Everything you tweet is an extension of your biz and your brand. If you want to scream about "getting thousands of followers," be my guest, but what's the funniest part about the above tweet? The actual guy has 149 followers. Seriously.

On Facebook, gluttony takes a different turn for me. While actually writing this book, a service provider that I am "friends" with sent me an invite to a Facebook event called *Freedom from the Fat Trap!!!* Really? One of two things happened here. She either sent the invitation, which wasn't even for her own event, to her entire friend list, or she specifically chose to invite me to the event. I am going to go ahead and guess that it is the former and that I also do not have to tell you how badly somebody could take this. It is about as bad as inviting somebody to an event called *You're Ugly and Here Is How You Can Look a Little Less Ugly*. Remember that everything you do impacts your business image, including inviting people to fat camp.

Sloth

Twitter is a conversation. It's truly what I love about it. But imagine having a conversation in person with someone where that person takes an hour to reply to you, face-to-face. How awkward would that be: "Hey, how's business?" and they blankly stare off for an hour, then reply "Good, thanks!" That's how it feels if someone takes a week to reply to a tweet. I once had someone who took 79 days to reply to a question that I asked her on Twitter. *Seventy-nine days*! If it takes you longer to reply than it would to walk over a handwritten reply to my home, you're doing it wrong. I know, not everyone is a tweetaholic like me, and not everyone can devote a good chunk of their day to Twitter. So if you have a limited amount of resources or time, let's say five hours a week, it's better to spend 45 minutes a day for the entire week than five hours once a week. Consistency breeds familiarity, which creates relationships.

Here we can combine Facebook and LinkedIn; if you are not going to be responsive on either site, then you probably shouldn't have a presence. There is a difference between being present and having a presence. You need to be active and responsive to people's requests, whether that is accepting people as contacts on LinkedIn or as friends on Facebook. I was guilty of this last year on LinkedIn when I recently went back to ramp things up and realized I had connection requests from eight months ago. How do you think it made those people feel?

Envy

Ya, I'm kind of a big deal on Twitter in my own mind, which at the end of the day means nothing to the majority of the world, but every day I get DMs[42] asking me to change my picture to add a "cause" or tweet about this or that. I'm all for causes, I'm a big charity guy, but mostly I'm a fan of choice, meaning it's your choice to support anything you want, but every once in a while people try to get others, through guilt, to change their avatar. When everyone changed their Twitter profile pictures to a shade of green to support some cause, I got asked daily why I hadn't changed mine yet. My answer to them? "It's none of your damn business why." My lack of participation in your cause does not infer lack of support, just like changing my avatar does not make me a better person by default. Same goes for people who think you should be obligated to follow them back if they follow you. Things on Twitter, just like most things in life, are choices. We should follow people based on interest, not out of courtesy.

The same goes for causes and groups on Facebook. You will see a popular cause of the month go around with plenty of invitations that you will usually ignore. Recently I had the pleasure of choosing to not join a cause just to be reinvited back multiple times by the same person. I admire their dedication but despise their persistence that has turned into annoyance.

One of LinkedIn's greatest functions is the endorsement, where people can give testimonials about your skills at a particular job. The system allows you to request endorsements from anyone in your contact list. This is okay if they actually worked with you or were customers; however, I frequently am requested to give endorsements for people who I barely know anything about; or

---

[42] DM is a Direct Message, which is a private message on Twitter that you can only send to someone who is following you.

they write in the request "if you endorse me then I will endorse you," which negates the very point of the system.

Wrath

One of the worst things about social media is the reactionary nature of it. Especially on Twitter, most of us don't think before tweeting, and for the most part it's okay because most tweets are harmless, boring, and innocent by nature. But once in a while we react or lash out beyond our better judgment. It takes a thousand tweets to build a reputation and one to change it all. Twitter feels intimate sometimes, like you're on an episode of *Friends*, having a conversation with a few people, except there are thousands lurking around. It's like having a harem of stalkers, without the creepiness.[43]

Being the object of someone's wrath is also common. For a full explanation on how to deal with trolls, check out the section about them later in the book. But in a nutshell: Don't feed them. They aren't owed a reply, your time, or your emotions. You're better than that.

Wrath can be even worse when it is cloaked in the disguise of being helpful. This is usually done by the spelling freaks or grammar police. I admit that I do not always proofread what I tweet—I barely proofread a blog post and then usually only after I have posted it. Posting on my public comments and implying that I am a moron because I spelled something wrong isn't in anybody's best interest. It makes me feel stupid and it makes you look bad. I was taught back in my human resource days that there was one rule: Praise in public and reprimand in private. So I would say praise in public and assist in private. If I asked for help or feedback in a public forum, then fire away, but if the spell-check is unsolicited, drop

---

[43] Okay, maybe a little creepiness.

me a note privately. It is actually appreciated and makes you look even better. But beware of those who ask for feedback in public as well—they are usually looking for praise.

Lust

Social media sites are filled with humans. And when you throw a bunch of humans into an environment, a few things are sure to be present: 20 percent of people will have bad breath, 30 percent will wonder how their hair looks, 60 percent like peanut butter and cheese sandwiches but are scared to say something (or maybe I'm the only one), and 100 percent will have hormones.[44] It happens. We can pretend they don't exist, but they're always there. It's one of the reasons to have a flattering picture as part of your social media profile; it catches the eye. The problem is when people turn creepy or obnoxious (and by people I mean guys). I'm truly blessed to know many incredible women on Twitter who are not only brilliant in business but attractive as well. The stories they tell me about direct messages or replies they get from some men make me shake my head. Seriously, folks, I'm not sure what book told you the line "Your lips look tasty" works, but it makes me picture *Silence of the Lambs*, and not for the cool stuff. Every tweet, every DM, represents your company, and more specifically you as a person.

It is even worse on Facebook, where the laidback attitude can make you look even worse. People post pictures of their vacations on the beach only to have some guy make a comment that totally ruins the entire thing. And I repeat that you are always marketing your business—every comment, every post, is an extension of your brand.

---

[44] By the way, I know that this doesn't equal 100 percent, so feel free to shoot me an e-mail to correct me.

Pride

You know what? Screw it. I have no problem with your being proud of something. I mean true pride. Something you accomplished, your kids, whatever. Scream it from the top of the mountains, good for you. Just do it in moderation. Don't just talk about yourself, spread pride of others, too. Retweet, comment, and share their accomplishments. One sin out of seven ain't so bad.

17

How Twitter Changed My Business

I'M NO STRANGER to social media or online social networking.[45] Ryze.com was one of the first business-oriented sites in the social networking universe, and I had built a nice network there both virtually and locally.

Fast-forward to April 2008 when I signed up at Twitter.com. I had heard about it from a few people and decided to throw my hat into the ring, but it didn't do much for me. I tweeted, read about how a few others were eating lunch or talking about their latest blog post, but nothing rocked my world. I used it casually until the end of that year. Then something changed.

I decided to give Twitter one last try. I had gotten up to around 2,000 followers and decided to give it my all for one month, to see if it really was a viable networking tool. So on January 1st, I took my own 30-day Twitter challenge. I would eat, breathe, and almost sleep on Twitter.[46] I added TwitterBerry to

---

[45] Back in the old days online, we used to call it "talking."
[46] We call that "Tweeting horizontally." I took a survey and the majority of mobile users check Twitter before going to bed and right when they wake up, while still in bed.

my BlackBerry, because it allowed me to access it on the go and tweet my heart out. At the end of the 30 days I was up to 10,000 followers and was hooked. I had made better and stronger relationships in that time span on Twitter than all the other social networking sites combined. I had built a loyal following, booked speaking engagements, and gained consulting clients, without ever pitching a thing.

At the time of writing the revised edition of this book, I have more than 100,000 followers, a best-selling book, and a massive network of incredible, smart, and funny business colleagues I never would have found otherwise. How did I get here? In those first 30 days, five things worked really well for me:

1. *Tweet constantly:* A single tweet has a short shelf-life—to create momentum you have to keep active. I wanted such a presence on Twitter that if I didn't tweet for a day or two, people would notice (and they did). It has to become a habit. Don't let the shortness of a tweet fool you into thinking it doesn't take any time to become known. You have to be present. I tweeted almost 7,000 times during those 30 days in January. Excessive? You bet. I don't recommend you try it. I was waiting for the A&E Intervention team to bust down my door to send me to rehab. But I got into the habit of being present on Twitter and got people into the habit of reading what I wrote. I had someone come up to me at an event and ask me how many times I tweet a day. When I replied a few hundred, she gasped and said, "Well, that's just too much! I would never follow you!" I wasn't exactly soul-crushed. It wasn't as if I was sending 200 text messages directly to my followers every day. Twitter is a current chat. You don't have to catch up; you don't have to read everything from everybody. You pop on, look around, and jump in. The same woman was wondering what kind of life I could have if I tweeted that much. A tweet

is shorter than a text message. I asked her how long it took her to send a text. She mentioned 10 to 20 seconds, which is longer than it takes me to send a tweet. It takes me roughly five to eight seconds to send a tweet. Even if it took me 10 seconds, I've now spent just more than a half hour sending those 200 tweets. Gasp! What a life I must live. There is no right amount to tweet. No one can tweet too much or too little because it's your account. You can't try to cater to certain followers because they don't like your frequency. When you have something to say, tweet it. When you see something of interest, reply to it. People will come and go, just keep pushing forward and focus on those who are with you.

2. *Tweet quality:* Every day I thought about what I could tweet that would be helpful to others. At first I tweeted a lot about business, and then I moved to specific Twitter tips because people were asking me what the best way was to do things. Replying to requests for help also connects you with people quickly. It gets you on their radar. Even now with tens of thousands of followers, I recognize the ones who jump in when I ask for help with something. Those are the people I can't wait to meet, and I don't have a problem with helping when they ask. It's part of that social currency. Give before you expect to get.

3. *Tweet retweetable content:* This goes along with tweeting quality. Not only did I try to think up tips daily, but I wrote them in less than 120 characters. Twitter allows up to 140 characters, but if someone wants to retweet it (RT) to show their followers, it adds to the original (i.e., they have to add "RT@UnMarketing" to the start of the tweet). The last thing I wanted people to have to do was to edit my tweet so it would fit. Why make people work to spread the word about you? Getting retweeted was the number-one thing that brought me new followers. Because they read the retweet from someone

they follow, it's like a mini-recommendation of me to them. I suggest writing three to five tips a day that are retweetable.[47]

4. *Be authentic:* It is just a fancy way of saying "be yourself." Twitter has a unique presence where people are connecting on a higher level than just a virtual business card. Give your opinion. Talk about your interests. Although entrepreneurs live their business 24 hours a day, it does not mean that they have to always talk business. I have met more fascinating business owners on Twitter talking about music or movies than about any business topic. When you can connect with others on non-business topics, it removes the impending threat of trying to sell to me. You actually want to get to know me? I'll join in with that!

5. *Use a face picture:* It is amazing when I log onto Twitter and up pops a tweet from someone I recognize. It's as if they just entered the room. I actually smile. When I see a tweet pop up with a logo as their picture, I don't get that feeling. It reminds me that this person has a business and is trying to sell me something. And unless you plan on walking around the networking event with your logo on your head, I won't recognize you when we meet in person. There is nothing better at an event than seeing someone you recognize, yet haven't met, and are already having that connection.

Also, make sure to use a good picture. It should not be an afterthought. You don't have to spend a truckload of money on a professional shoot, but the faded Polaroid from 1986 of you and your dog isn't going to cut it.[48] Twitter is like online dating for business. It's awkward when you use a picture from 20 years

---

[47] This also inspired me to write a song. You can hear it at RetweetMeVideo.com. I really should have inserted a "best of" CD with every book purchase but feared that people would pop it into their car stereo and scar their children for life.

[48] Also, avoid the "hand under the chin" pose. It's just awkward. Are you listening real estate agents?

ago that looks nothing like you now. I used to use a picture that was about eight years old, mainly because it was from a photo shoot and made me look like a GQ model[49] with a serious model pose[50] and no smile at all. This wasn't me, but I thought it made me look good. I soon changed to a candid shot from a photographer friend[51] with me smiling, mid-conversation. That's exactly how I look, and there is no "Whoa, that's not what I expected" when I show up at an event.

A word about automation: You may be tempted to use automation to keep a presence on Twitter when you're not around, but I advise against it. Twitter is a conversation; people think it's you talking. If you use a third-party program to automatically tweet for you when you're not around, it's like sending a mannequin to a networking event in your place with a Post-it note attached. It's not authentic; it says that you want people to listen to you but not vice versa. A colleague of mine tweeted about his upcoming workshop, and a few people replied with questions about it but got no answer. Why? I knew for a fact that he was on a cruise for a week without access. How do you think he looked after that? It sends the wrong message to your followers, and it's not worth it. For further proof, there are multiple examples of conferences that have a screen up with live tweets from people using the conference #hashtag where the speaker is on stage, and a tweet comes up from them. While they are speaking. And not on Twitter.[52]

People give a lot of reasons why they feel automation is okay. They will tell you that automation allows you to reach people in different time zones, allows you to make Twitter scalable, and you get to build relationships when you aren't around. Please do not

---

[49] Minus the good looks, body, and money.

[50] Picture the "Blue Steel" pose from Zoolander.

[51] www.CouchSurfingOri.com.

[52] Bonus points if the speaker talks about "authenticity" or being "true."

listen to them! Automating tweets means that you want people to listen to you, but you are unwilling to listen to them. There is no such thing as automated engagement. There is no such thing as programmed authenticity. You must realize that this is not a good idea. It is not the first tweet that builds the relationship. It is the conversation that comes afterward. It is a different story if your account is a feed of events/news and that is what people follow you for. The problem is when people think you are tweeting to them and you are not really there.

There are also sites that will notify you when someone unfollows you and the tweet you sent that did it. I shudder thinking about it. Why would you want that? Do you like emotional pain? Do you really want to know every time someone leaves you? People have justified it by saying it can help you see why people leave so you can tweak how you tweet. Ugh. Why would you change for people who've left when the people who stay are there because of how you are? People unfollow for different reasons. Don't care about them.

And the daddy of all automation: the auto-follow. Like any tool that becomes successful for businesses, there will always be people looking for shortcuts. Because human nature dictates that everything is a numbers game, people want to build up a massive following on Twitter. But who actually wants to spend the time it takes to build real relationships? In comes automation! These systems will follow 500 or so people a day for you with the prediction that the majority of them will follow you back. Then the system drops either the people who didn't follow back or everyone all together, making it look like you have a lot of followers but only follow a few yourself. I don't even know where to begin with how wrong this is, especially in a forum like Twitter where authenticity is everything. It's not about how many followers you have but your engagement with them. Don't look to build quantity, build quality. I started at zero followers and have grown it out of engagement, one person at a time.

18

Tassimo

JUSTIFYING SOCIAL MEDIA is easy to do for marketing consultants like me. My clients are usually ready and willing to embrace the power of engaging with their community. This isn't the case when it comes to large corporations that are so used to the old style of marketing that it sometimes almost takes a miracle to help them see the new way of doing things.

Kraft Canada was a different story when Duri Al-Ajrami, the director of social marketing for Ogilvy Canada, approached them. He knew that the power of social media would work incredibly well in getting the word out about the new Tassimo single-cup hot beverage brewing system that Kraft was about to launch in Canada.

The easy way to do things would have been to simply do what any company has always done and invest millions in a TV ad campaign and hope that within all the noise somebody would hear you. It always baffles me to see companies fight for better ways to air commercials when consumers are thinking about better ways to avoid commercials.

Duri persisted with the client and was willing to prove that it would work. Ogilvy and Kraft monitored the conversation about coffee in general, their special brand, and their competitors. Their goal was to exponentially grow the conversation about this new machine without clouding the airways with unwanted commercials. Due to budget constraints, they were unable to use mass TV advertising and instead purchased 1,000 machines to give away to influential people in social media in Canada. I was one of those people.

The way that I was approached is a lesson in itself on how to approach bloggers or influential social media people. After using some tools through Radian6, a company that identified who the key people were, Duri sent individual, personalized e-mails to each person. I get many e-mails from people who want me to review their books—scratch that, promote their books—and I never get more than a form letter. Duri was different. His e-mail was personal to me because we both live in the same town, and he mentioned a few things I was talking about online, which showed me he actually did some research. He was upfront with me in the e-mail, letting me know he was getting in touch with certain influencers in social media and was wondering if I would like one of the new Tassimo coffee systems for free. In return, if I wanted to, I could review it honestly or tweet about it, and although most companies wouldn't like it, he requested that I be as honest as I could. Not one to pass up free stuff, because if I don't like it then it would make a great regift, I said sure, send it over. We also continued the conversation over e-mail and made plans at a later date to have lunch and discuss marketing in general because we both had a passion for social media.

A week or so later, I received not only the machine but also nine different boxes of "T DISCS" that contained different types of coffee, tea, and hot chocolate so I could try them all out. You have to understand something here: I may be the laziest man in the history of all time. I don't like making pots of coffee mostly because of the effort and how it goes stale really quickly. When I looked at this machine and how it promised to make great coffee quickly one cup at a time, I knew I had found my new best friend. Sure enough, this thing rocked the Casbah. It actually ended up reducing the amount of time I went out to pick up coffee because it was so good and quick. So, of course, I started tweeting about it, as did many others.

The following week I received another e-mail from Duri. It wasn't an e-mail requesting that I review the machine, as you might think. You know the old "Okay, we gave you something, now give us something" type of e-mail; he was actually writing to ask me to pick 10 other people who I thought would appreciate receiving a machine as well. Now I am Santa Claus! He made it clear in the e-mail that the people I recommended were not going to be just suggestions—the 10 people I named would all get a machine themselves. The only request was that they also have a social media presence.[53] So, as you can probably guess, the people I selected were ecstatic and were really anticipating receiving their machines.

The strategy was brilliant on many different levels, but the key to it working was having a great product to talk about. The machine is unique and buzz-worthy; I don't think this method would work as well with toilet paper.[54] The buzz about the machine was not only incredible, it was measurable. Right before the campaign started, in October 2009, Tassimo was being talked about only 0.04 percent of the time in conversations around coffeemakers and coffee social habits in Canada. By December 2009, Tassimo had reached 12.6 percent of conversations, being mentioned almost 5,000 times online versus around 50 times

---

[53] So, now you know, Mom, this is why you didn't get one. I told you that you should be on Twitter.

[54] Unless it had some kind of auto-wipe feature. If you represent a company that has come up with this idea, please get in touch with me. I would like to try it, along with 10 influential friends.

before the campaign. Their two competitors, which stayed with classic old-school marketing, had numbers that remained flat in the conversation, no increase or decrease, both having less than 1 percent the entire time.

Overall sales have been higher than expected for the machine and the coffee discs. I am sure that if you actually look closely, I account for half of them. ☺ My kitchen is filled with boxes of T DISCS, although my son is tired of daddy asking if he wants to try a new latte flavor that just came out, but he won't pass up another hot chocolate.

The biggest knock on social media is not being able to get measurable results, but as you can see, you not only can get real results, you can generate real conversations.

19

Local Twitter

"WELL, TWITTER IS good for you, Scott. Your market can be anywhere in the world." And so it begins. Another reason given why a business claims it doesn't need to engage with its marketplace by using social media.

Whenever I speak to geographically based businesses, we always end up talking about whether Twitter and other sites are valuable when your customers are all close by. For example, why would a pizza place in Dallas care about connecting with someone in Toronto?

Fair enough. I do understand that when most of your customers are within the range of local transit that they should be your first focus for marketing. However, connecting on a large scale with people in the same industry outside of your competitive geographic area is a smart thing to do. It allows you to share best practices and solve problems without taking away local market share.

If your business is local, there are four things you can do to help you focus your Twitter efforts:

1. *Use a keyword location-specific search in Twitter for people in your area.* Many people suggest using keyword terms to search for

potential customers, but it doesn't work well for a local business. When you put the name of your city or town into the search with your business type, the tweets that come up would have to include both (i.e., I need a massage in Toronto versus I need a massage). Such a specific search may not be fruitful, so the way to solve this issue on Twitter is to do a search using the term *near*. By putting "near:Toronto" beside your keyword, you will see all the tweets from people who listed in their profile location that they are near Toronto. So now the person who tweets "I want a pizza" can be found geographically. Use either the "search" bar on the right side of Twitter or Search .Twitter.com.

Now just you wait!

This isn't an excuse to start replying to everyone on this list to say "*Come use us! We rulez teh universse!* LOLZ!" Reply to some people, say something like, "Heya, we could help you out! Let us know, hope u feel better soon!"

I'm not done with you!

Please do not set up an auto-reply system that will send replies to anyone who mentions a certain word in a tweet. Seriously, I will hunt you down and give you a stink-eye of epic proportions. These people have potentially raised their hands, and the last thing you need to do is hit them up with a prewritten auto-tweet and then when they check out your profile, all they see is that same tweet to hundreds of others. Doesn't make them feel all warm and fuzzy.

Most importantly, this tool should be used to see people in your area to start engaging. Actually care about them. Get to know them. You're a person, and amazingly, so are they! Set up this search in a program like TweetDeck so it automatically refreshes the search.

2. *Use Twitter Grader to find the best users in your area.* Twitter Grader ranks users by awesomeness (my word), not just by

follower count. Use its location search so you can find the best users in your area to get to know. Same rule applies here: Don't follow just to send them ads. Engage, get to know people. It's like a live networking event, except you can't be cornered by the creepy dude drinking scotch.

3. *Twellow Pages: It's like the Yellow Pages but people actually use it.* Using its search function, you can search by interests and by location. This is a great site for finding people in specific industries. Make sure that you also list your own Twitter account in the directory under the "Register for Free" link on the homepage.

4. *Tell them you're there!* It sounds silly, but tell people that you're on Twitter. Put it in the company newsletter, in ads, at the checkout. You'd be amazed how many people are on Twitter, and if they like you they can spread the word to others in the Twitter world.

We now know that Twitter is an amazing tool for local business. Location-based social media is happening today and certain to be a big part of the future online. With smartphones in almost everyone's hands, GPS, Google maps, and sites like Twitter and Facebook creating online communities, more and more we let the world know where we are. I like to think of it as reverse stalking. Recently, there are programs dedicated to just this function.

Sites like FourSquare and Gowalla have the sole purpose of telling the world where you are. These have some amazing potential and also dangers for businesses. Location-based technology allows restaurants to dynamically let potential customers know their menu and specials. Passersby can find out where the best coffee shop is as recommended by their trusted circle and then let the world know they are there and "love the coffee, great service" and so on. At conferences, we can find our friends, set up meetings, and read reviews of venues all in one place, and then add our two cents to the dialogue.

The danger to local businesses is the same as with any form of social media. You do not control the message. If your product is bad, if your service is lacking, if the store down the road is more active and engaging, then your business is going to suffer. For the individual, again as in social media in general, location-based tagging and check-ins add another dimension that can hurt your personal brand. Remember, if you let the world know that you are someplace they think you shouldn't be, it will not be without consequences.

My biggest issue with banking on people telling others where they are is that for the most part women[55] don't like the idea. I, being a semi-egotistical male,[56] don't mind that people know where I am all the time, but rarely have I explained location-based social media and had a woman reply, "Awesome! Let's tell the world where I am!" Also, when you are telling the world where you are, you are also telling them where you aren't (i.e., at home). Social media allows people to come into our lives, but location-based media is a little much for most people.

---

[55] I truly believe that women drive social media. The majority of men are taught to climb the ladder of success, where only one person can be on each rung. But women, almost by default, understand community and would rather take an elevator up with others. Poetic and prejudice at the same time, I know.

[56] Is there any other kind? Heyooooo!

20

Domino's — Word of Mouth

Mouths Are Moving . . .

DURING A BAD storm in April 2009, Amy Ravit Korin decided to order a few pizzas, because cooking wasn't on her evening agenda. She decided to place an order online with Domino's, getting through the entire process without talking to a single human being. You might then assume that this would make the order seamless and error-free, because she typed in exactly what she wanted. This was not the case. The order was not only wrong but it was late, taking more than an hour to arrive. So, being the social media lover and consultant that she is, she hopped onto Twitter to let her feelings about this experience be known.

Much to her surprise, a little while later she received a tweet back from Ramon De Leon, who owns multiple locations of Domino's in the Chicago area. He acknowledged her tweet and promised to make it right. She was already waiting for a new pizza to replace the wrong one, so she figured short of a coupon that this would be the end of it. Little did she know what was about to happen.

She woke up the next day to a video[57] that was made for her by Ramon as well as Junior, the store manager of the specific location she had ordered from. This is perhaps the best $2\frac{1}{2}$-minute video any business owner could see. It has both of Domino's reps apologizing for what happened, not making up any excuses, and you can truly see the passion behind their words—that they really do want to make it right. Amy was quite taken aback when she saw this video. She doesn't have a million followers, she isn't Ashton Kutcher, she was simply one dissatisfied customer. Keyword here is *was*. After seeing the video, she forwarded it to others and it caught on like wildfire. The video to date has been viewed more than 100,000 times around the world. Sadly, one of the reasons it has been viewed so many times is that it is so rare for companies to own their mistakes. When people complain to you, they are first looking for validation, not compensation. They want to know that they have been heard, they want to know that they matter, and they want to know that you care.

Ramon acknowledged her as quickly as possible on Twitter, which never would have happened in the first place if he hadn't understood that word of mouth happens with or without him. He took a negative and turned it into an exponential positive. If I told you that I had a room full of current potential customers all talking about your products and your competitors, would you not show up? Not listening and then acting on social media chatter is like not showing up at all. The only thing worse is to have a presence in social media and only talk and not listen. It would be like showing up in the room with earplugs on.

For you to hear what people are saying about your company is simple. Run a search on Twitter by using your company name. There are also tools you can use to make this search easier, such as setting up custom columns on TweetDeck, a free Google alert

---

[57] See the actual video here: http://bit.ly/aLxfGA

setup for your keywords, and a service like Radian6, which is a tool to listen to, measure, and engage with your market across all social media sites. You can also use these same tools to keep on top of what your competition is doing and what people are saying about them.

Ramon ended up making things right by showing up to an event that Amy was a part of, not only because he happened to be catering it, but so that he and Junior could drop off a personal pizza for her along with a dozen roses.

21

Naked Pizza

In 2006 Naked Pizza opened its doors in New Orleans with a mission to make an unhealthy food healthier. Naked Pizza claims to make the world's healthiest pizza. The crust is made of 12 whole grains, low-fat mozzarella, and an additive-free tomato sauce. And from what I have heard, it is pretty darn tasty. The company's pizzas are 100 percent natural and gluten-free, so people with a condition (such as celiac disease) who cannot have wheat can still enjoy their pizza.

In March 2009 Mark Cuban, owner of the Dallas Mavericks and a gazillionaire,[58] advised Jeff Leach, cofounder of the pizza place, to get on Twitter. The owners wanted to create a virtual but local presence that would not only engage their marketplace but reduce the typically high cost of marketing that goes along with the pizza industry. They tested out their first Twitter-only promotion the following month on April 23, 2009.[59] The promotion brought in 15 percent of total sales for the day. The best part is

---

[58] Or a billionaire, let's just say he has more money than I do.

[59] It's also my birthday, which they failed to mention in their promotions. I will let that slide. Once.

that 90 percent of those sales were new customers. One of the concerns with using a new type of marketing channel like Twitter is that if you sold 100 units of something on Twitter, it doesn't mean much if all you do is cannibalize business you would have gotten anyway, which is why the 90 percent of orders to new customers is significant. On May 29, the pizza place owners decided to try another campaign. This one generated almost 75 percent of their record-selling day—directly from people calling from Twitter.

The owners went as far as removing their old billboard that posted their phone number to call for delivery and changed it to, "Twitter follow us for specials www.Twitter.com/NakedPizza." They have also added a kiosk in the store, inviting customers to sign up for Twitter and to follow them.

I spoke to Robbie Vitrano, chief brand designer and cofounder of Naked Pizza,[60] when doing research for the book, and he kind of surprised me with how much he got social media. And I don't mean that I was expecting him to be an idiot. It's just that he comes from an agency background, which is usually about mass-market push messages. He really emphasized the point that he was more than happy that most companies were missing the boat when it came to social media, because their loss was Naked Pizza's gain. It was also encouraging to hear that he had such passion behind the product and that the company as a whole was not afraid to show its passion in its blog.[61] These guys take a stand on many issues because they are trying to redefine pizza away from its image as a food that has contributed to the obesity epidemic in the world. They make no bones about why they think things like Crohn's and celiac diseases have been on the rise and what they should and shouldn't be doing about them. That is a powerful stance, even though it repels some people who also happen to be their target market.

---

[60] Jeff Leach, Randy Crochet, and Brock Fillinger are the other cofounders.

[61] www.blog.nakedpizza.biz

22

Don't Feed the Trolls

NEGATIVE THINGS CAN happen when you become active on social media sites. I am not going to lie to you. I have made myself visible on these sites, and I know what can happen—the good and the bad. When you jump into the social media world for your company, you invite the world to come. And all the world does.

Back in my über-geek days, I used to hang out in IRC chat rooms. These rooms were places where fellow geeks could hang out in different topic-based rooms, swap stories, MP3s,[62] and generally connect with others.

Every time, bar none, he would appear—the troll:

In Internet slang, a troll is someone who posts controversial, inflammatory, irrelevant, or off-topic messages in an online community, such as an online discussion forum, chat room, or blog, with the primary intent of provoking other users into an

---

[62] Back in the day when MP3 stood for "I'm pirating music, take that establishment!"

emotional response or of otherwise disrupting normal on-topic discussion.[63]

Usually, this sorry excuse for a human being would type something like "Your mom is hot" or "That's what your mom said."[64] Nowadays, trolls have moved into the social media stream, leaving nasty blog comments, sending meathead tweets or insulting Facebook comments. Witness a recent tweet from someone:

"Am I the only one to find @unmarketing[65] an annoying, blabber mouthed, self prophetic ass?"

I had to look-up "self-prophetic." How do you deal with them? How do I deal with them?[66] Here are four tips to get you out of the troll spiral:

1. *DFTT (Don't Feed the Trolls)*. This is by far the best piece of advice I ever received back in the day, and it still holds true. I was getting grumpy about a guy baiting me in a chat, and someone sent me a private message with that line. Trolls feel horrible about their lives, their haircuts, and are angry that a bowtie has not become acceptable attire in society. And they are hungry. If you don't feed them, they eventually go look for food elsewhere.
2. *Don't expose them*. I'll admit, my first reaction to these morons was to reply back with my sharp wit, but never forget this: If they tweet something to you, only their followers will see it

---

[63] http://en.wikipedia.org/wiki/Troll_(Internet).

[64] The irony of this is that the troll usually resides in his mom's basement and is horribly, horribly alone.

[65] That's my Twitter ID, just in case you want to call me names, too.

[66] And why am I asking myself questions? Soon I'll be referring to myself in the third person. Scott doesn't do that though.

(and they usually have 20 followers, my mom not being one of them, contrary to their apparent liking of said mom). *But* if you reply, if you take the bait, you now have the tweet on your main profile page, feeding the troll exponentially! Not only do you give them the satisfaction of being fed, but you've also given them a platform to be exposed to all your followers. The tweet above was sent to me yesterday. I didn't reply, I just blocked and went on with my day. Sure, I don't like seeing it, but I found it kind of funny and it isn't entirely false. ☺

3. *Pick who gets your emotional currency.* You only have so much emotion to go around. It should be spent on people who value it, who value you, and not someone who just finished a 36-hour bender on "World of Warcraft" and is angry that his wizard lost an epic battle on the island of Corinthian. There are way too many incredible people in this world, and on Twitter especially, who are worth your time.

4. *Realize where they're aiming.* It is the troll's lack of self-esteem that brews the hate. It actually has nothing to do with you. Does the troll know you? Does he have tea and crumpets with you? No. So screw 'em.

This isn't about living in a bubble and only listening to happy things. Constructive criticism is one thing, but being a jerk is another. You're worth more than troll bait. Don't listen, don't acknowledge. Just be you, and do it at the highest level possible, because I think you rule.

23

Tweetathon

As YOU HAVE probably figured out by now, if you didn't already know before picking up this book, I love Twitter. Not just because it makes up for my lack of popularity in high school, but for all the incredible people I've met since joining it. It has restored my faith in humanity. No other events have proven this more to me than Tweetathons.

A Tweetathon borrows in concept from the traditional fundraising telethon, but it takes place on Twitter. The online event usually benefits one charity and takes place in a set period of time. Some Tweetathons enlist celebrities to help spread the word, while some offer prizes. Others focus on raising the number of followers for an organization's Twitter account and accept pledges for every 100 new followers within the time period. Like many social media fundraising tactics, the key is to be original—there are no rules!

All you need is a Twitter account with a high number of engaged followers, or a group of people willing to tweet on your behalf, and a way to accept donations.

I have organized multiple Tweetathons that have raised upwards of $50,000. Here are my nine key areas that led to their success:

1. *Organizer span of influence.* In order to be successful with a Tweetathon, you need to have preexisting networks of supporters or influencers who can help. You can't just open an account on Twitter and start asking for donations. Twitter is a community, a conversation, not a pitch platform.

2. *The cause.* Choose a cause or program that everyone can relate to, not just a select few. People donate and share causes that move them.

3. *The raffle.* The Tweetathons provided an entry into a prize raffle for each donation. Most of the raffle prizes were donated by people I'd previously connected with on Twitter. Some of the donations didn't come from manufacturers, but from friends who just went out and bought prizes because they wanted to be a part of it all. I was able to get these awesome donations because of all the social currency I have on Twitter (see point #1). I had built a relationship with almost everyone who donated an item for the raffle. This was not the goal of being on Twitter or getting to know them, it was just the result, but it is so incredible what happens when you ask for help from virtual friends—people step up to the plate.

4. *The set donation suggestion.* There were two suggested donation levels set for the Tweetathons. The first was $12 and included one entry into the raffle, and the second level was $120 and got donors 10 entries and a complimentary website review.

5. *The short timeframe.* You need to create a sense of excitement and urgency, and a deadline can help make this happen. People should want to donate now and pass it along to their network right away.

6. *The amount of tweets*. During a Tweetathon, I would tweet almost every minute, driving people back to the donation page. A single tweet lasts a minute or two on people's radars, tops. If you want to stay in front of people, you have to keep tweeting.

7. *The social proof retweet*. I retweeted donation tweets, adding a thank you. I really wanted people to feel how appreciated their time and donation was. Retweets and thank yous increase exposure and can lead to campaigns becoming trending topics.[67]

8. *Cause soldiers*. We can call the Tweetathon supporters a Tweeting Army. A Tweetathon is really a community event. It isn't about one person, but a network of supporters sharing a cause with their networks.

9. *Focus*. The only call-to-action for the Tweetathon was to donate. Recently I've seen live streaming video, interviews, and musical acts that take away from the donation focus. Their heart is in the right place, but if people are busy listening to an interview subject talk about a topic outside of the fundraiser, they get distracted and eventually click away. If you still want to have virtual events during the fundraiser, at the very least have a banner across it always reminding people of why they're there. Make the donate button (or ChipIn widget)[68] at the very top or alongside the video that is being used.

Twitter can be a great tool for causes and charities. It's all about starting with a cause people care about, finding a strong, connected platform of voices to spread the word, and making it simple and easy for people to donate and be a part of the event.

---

[67] A trending topic is something that many people are tweeting about. The top ones make it onto the Twitter homepage, which then exposes it to a whole new audience
[68] Chipin.com is a free tool you can use to monitor the progress of donations.

24

Your Website—Old School versus New School

THE HUB OF most businesses—the website—is the most poorly done thing of them all. After reviewing countless sites, most were guilty of the same old-school mistakes.

Brochure versus Hub

More than half of the websites I reviewed had nothing to give, only to buy. No information to learn, the sites were simply digital brochures. Where are you aiming on that pyramid? If it's just to sell stuff, keep doing this: buy or good-bye. But your website should be the hub of your business—the place where people can go to learn about you and to learn content.

Give away some knowledge. People fear that if they give it away, people won't need to hire or buy from them. If everything you know about your industry can be explained in a few articles, you don't know much. It's not just knowledge that people buy from you, it's the application of the knowledge for their specific situation. This is why a blog-driven site comes in handy. The nature of a blog is the sharing of knowledge unconditionally.

You don't have to post every day or even every week. Although frequency helps, consistent quality content is more important. I would rather you write three great posts in a month than 10 mediocre ones.

Pitch versus Authenticity Newsletters

I see people doing this all the time. I sign up for their "newsletter" and all I get are pitches for products. I want to learn from you, that's why I signed up. I made this mistake years ago myself. I built a newsletter up to more than 300,000 subscribers and started my pitches. I lost more than 100,000 subscribers in six months. Ya, whoops. The gurus talk about "open rates" in ways that they tell you to make compelling, even misleading headlines[69] to get people to open your newsletter. I've seen subject lines with "Scott, this is personal," and when I open it, it's just their newsletter, which is really a pitch for a product they're launching. For fun[70] I created an e-mail address to just sign up 25 "marketing guru" newsletters to see how much content I would actually get, compared to pitches. You guessed it, none. Every edition from every person was a pitch. Many were pitches for each other's product launches, taken from the same template. Two of them teach "authentic marketing." Go directly to jail, do not pass *Go*, and I'm unsubscribing. The majority of the newsletters also used different styles of misleading subject lines. I don't mean creative ones that pique your interest; I mean blatant deception like "I'm leaving the Internet" or my favorite, "Sorry, we sold out!" just to get you to open the e-mail to see, "That subject line is something I don't want to have to send you, since we're almost sold out!"

---

[69] And for those who use ALL CAPS in subject lines, or a fake "RE:" to get me to open it, you have a special place waiting for you.

[70] This is my idea of fun. I need counseling.

It's not about list size, open rates, or click-throughs if all you're going to do is pitch your subscribers. It's about engagement. It's about when I see your newsletter in my inbox, among 400 other things in the morning, I say to myself, "I *have* to read this, it's always great." How many newsletters can you say that about? Are people saying that about yours?

Don't make people angry. They talk about it when they're angry. They tell others about it when they're angry. And if you say, "Well, at least they're talking about me!" I'm going to slug you right in the gut.[71]

Your newsletter should be an authentic representation of what the people signed up for and what the content is going to offer. If they signed up for tips on how to be better parents, then send them tips on how to be a better parent!

If the unfortunate occurs and someone wants to unsubscribe to your newsletter, please make sure that you use a system that makes it easy for that person and is quick to remove. This alone can ensure that an unsatisfied reader does not turn into a livid unsubscriber. Not only are easy unsubscribes good karma, it is also part of the CAN-SPAM Act. You have to allow people to unsubscribe.

When I tried to unsubscribe from the Harry & David newsletter, I remembered that, because I am a past customer, the company does not actually fall under the CAN-SPAM Act. But because it took me three seconds to sign up for their newsletter, it should take the same amount of effort to remove me. This was not the case. When I went to change my settings and submitted them, the message said it would take 7 to 10 business days to complete my request. Nothing short of building an ark should take 7 to 10 business days, let alone a virtual function of removing a name from a database that was added instantly.

---

[71] And then refund the book to you. You're too dumb to continue reading this. The ALL CAPS people are waiting for you.

Originally, I just didn't want the newsletter because they were sending it daily and I had no need for information about gift baskets so frequently, but this just made them look silly. Every point of contact is a point of engagement—it either heightens the relationship or lowers it, even doing something as trivial as this task.

Static versus Dynamic

This comes down to a lack of creativity. A static website is a lack of new products. In the old days, when you put up a website you put up a few articles that sat there. No dates on them, no comments, just words in virtual concrete. It actually gave us an excuse not to update our content because the date was not listed from the last post. Today, a reader can use a blog post date to see how committed you are to content. Ever-growing content pays off in positioning; an engaging ad even helps with search engines.

Coming up with new content—and even more so, new products—seems to be a hurdle for people. But I don't blame people for it. We suffer from one of two things usually: perfection paralysis or consumption overload.

Perfection paralysis is when we are afraid to come out with something as simple as a blog post all the way to a big product because it's not "perfect." That's even something I'm guilty of when I wrote this book. What if I leave something out? What if I'm wrong?[72] We all know the phrase "no one's perfect," but forget it when it comes to us. I'm not suggesting that you release half-finished products or unfinished blog posts, but once you've given it your all, it's time to let it out there. Nothing will ever be perfect, and that's why software has releases like 2.0. If you're stumped on what method to use to deliver a product (e.g., audio, video, ebook),

---

[72] Not likely, but it's minutely possible. ☺

ask your list! Survey your list, give people a reason to answer,[73] and they will pick the method for you.

Consumption overload is when we never stop buying learning tools. We buy the next great ebook/DVD series of how to succeed in business, and then the next, while never actually implementing any of the ideas. Do this for yourself: Stop buying learning materials[74] for one week and put into practice one new item you've learned recently. The best ideas in the world aren't the profitable ones, but the best-implemented ideas are.

Our Site versus Your Site

Yes, it's your company website, but it doesn't mean that everything has to be about you. On your "About Us" page, knock yourself out with the self-congratulatory speak, but I don't care about you until I know you understand and care about me. The best example of this is when I sign up for your newsletter. The two typical responses given when someone subscribes are:

1. Thanks for signing up for our newsletter. Your request has been processed; you will receive the next edition when it comes out. 9589203-293844[75]
2. You've signed up for our newsletter. We rule. Look at what you are entitled to buy from us right away. Click on one of the 10 product links below! Thanks!

The first response, the generic confirmation, doesn't exactly make me sit on the edge of my seat in anticipation for the next

---

[73] For the chance to win a $50 Amazon.com gift card, I got 11,000-plus replies to a survey from a list of 100,000.

[74] Unless you're reading this in the bookstore, debating to purchase it. Then buy this book first. Ha ha. No really, buy it. You can't use this advice without buying it. It's somewhere in the FTC guidelines, I'm sure of it.

[75] The generic e-mail form number is always a classy touch. Almost as sweet as saying {INSERT FIRST NAME HERE} and not doing it properly.

edition. The second one sets the tone for what I'll be receiving in the future: sales pitches and sales pitches disguised as articles.

Where is the logic here? Your potential customers raise their hands to say they trust you enough to want to learn from you, and you send them that? Engage with them. I know you can't handcraft every thank-you personally, but even with automation you can have an engagement touch. Here's what you'll receive if you sign up over at Un-Marketing.com:

Subject: Thanks for signing up, may I ask . . .
Hi there,
Thanks for signing up to the UnMarketing newsletter. I know how an inbox can get crowded and I appreciate you allowing my newsletter to get through the clutter. May I ask what line of business you're in? It helps me tailor the newsletter to you even better.
Sincerely,
Scott Stratten, President
www.Un-Marketing.com

I get at least 40 percent of subscribers replying to it. Half of them even say, "I know this is an automated welcome but just wanted to say it's a nice touch!"

I've started countless conversations with subscribers from this method alone. Even if you don't reply to every single one, it gives you a great feel for your list. The gold isn't in the list anymore, it's in the engagement.

I'm Great versus You're Great

We know that you think you know what you're doing, but do others? The majority of business websites had no testimonials at all from satisfied customers. The old school of thought is that people will give them when they feel like it, but many people are happy to provide one if you just ask. If you are a B2B[76] provider, you can also offer a link back to that company's website. When you're good, you tell people. When you're great, others say it for you. Let the business owners know that you don't need to provide their full personal name if they don't want it used, but the more info you can show, the better.

Note: In October 2009 the Federal Trade Commission (FTC) changed the guidelines for endorsements. Please check to ensure that you are in compliance. Everything from social media to ads is impacted. Just search "FTC testimonials" online to get updated details. In a nutshell from the FTC site:

> Under the revised Guides, advertisements that feature a consumer and convey his or her experience with a product or service as typical when that is not the case will be required to clearly disclose the results that consumers can generally expect. In contrast to the 1980 version of the Guides—which allowed advertisers to describe unusual results in a testimonial as long as they included a disclaimer such as 'results not typical'—the revised Guides no longer contain this safe harbor.

> The revised Guides also add new examples to illustrate the longstanding principle that "material connections" (sometimes payments or free products) between advertisers and endorsers—connections that consumers would not expect—must be disclosed. These examples address what constitutes an endorsement when the message is conveyed by bloggers or other "word-of-mouth" marketers. The revised Guides specify that while decisions will be reached on a case-by-case basis, the post of a blogger who receives cash or in-kind payment to review a product is considered an

---

[76] Business to Business as opposed to Business to Consumer.

endorsement. Thus, bloggers who make an endorsement must disclose the material connections they share with the seller of the product or service. Likewise, if a company refers in an advertisement to the findings of a research organization that conducted research sponsored by the company, the advertisement must disclose the connection between the advertiser and the research organization. And a paid endorsement—like any other advertisement—is deceptive if it makes false or misleading claims.[77]

You don't want to be on the FTC's bad side, so please consult somebody 100 times smarter than me to be sure you're within the guidelines.

A Jungle versus a Map

When people land on your website, they will feel as if they have arrived at the right place, or they might be overwhelmed and click away. Too many choices are not a good thing when it comes to your site visitors. On average, the sites we looked at had 25 different choices to click on from their homepage. *Average was 25!!* That means many had even more![78] Have a look at your site. Is it logical what actions you're hoping visitors will do? Is it easy to find things? If your main goal, outside of providing great content, is to get people into your pull-and-stay mechanism, such as a newsletter, is that an obvious thing for them to do? Does it call out from the page? I don't mean in an obnoxious, animated GIF[79] sort of way, but does it attract the eye enough for someone to look into it?

---

[77] www.ftc.gov/opa/2009/10/endortest.shtm.

[78] The record was 96 click options. Sweet mother of ADD, what do you want a visitor to do other than to run away screaming?

[79] Popular in the late 1990s, animated GIFs were used to show sites that were "Under Construction" or for the designer to use the newest, coolest thing. Same applies to the flash intros you see on sites today. Ugh.

Then you need to give me a reason to sign up for your newsletter/ updates. The most popular method when surveying these sites was:

Sign up for our newsletter!

Really? Was the exclamation point the thing that was supposed to get me interested in signing up? Like I'm on the borderline, still a little hesitant, and then I saw it and said "Crikey! They're pretty jacked-up about their newsletter! I gotta get me some of this!" No one needs another newsletter. No one needs "your" newsletter. People always want useful information. Throw me a bone. Why should I sign up? Will you be providing weekly tips on how to save my business money? Then say it. Make your website clean looking, clear so I know where I need to go, and if I choose to take that next step with you, follow through with what you said you'd provide.

A word about external links: Linking to other useful content outside of your website is not only fine, it's a great idea. There are even great reasons to do so when it comes to search engine rankings. However, when you do provide a link, make sure that when your visitors click on it, they are taken to the site in a new browser window. If you refer to a post on someone else's blog and it changes to their site in the same window, you've lost them. It's one simple line of code within the link to do it.[80]

High versus Low Barrier to Engagement

We've all seen it. You like what you see on a site, go to sign up for their newsletter/blog updates, and they ask for your name, e-mail, state, phone, favorite Bon Jovi[81] tune, and your mother's maiden name. I've asked site owners countless times why they ask for so much when all they need is an e-mail address and maybe first

---

[80] "target=_blank" in HTML code. Ya, learned basic HTML in 1995. You should see how many animated GIFs I could put on one page.

[81] *Livin' on a Prayer*, or *Blaze of Glory* from his solo career.

name for personalization? They always respond, "It gives me great demographic info for my subscribers." I can't argue with that, it certainly does. What the owners don't realize is that for every single new thing you ask for, you lose a percentage of people who were going to subscribe. We've run multiple tests, and something as simple as asking for first and last name greatly reduced sign-ups compared to first name only. And don't get me started on requesting a phone number. What do you think I'll be saying to myself if I see you're asking for that? "These guys are gonna phone me, no thanks."

I understand that in some industries when you request something of value for free (white papers, etc.) it's standard to ask for everything, and it makes sense. You're giving something of high value away, and the recipient knows it and doesn't have an issue in letting you know who they are fully. But for a simple newsletter, you scare away more value than you'd ever retain by asking for too much.

When it comes to single opt-in (enter e-mail address and you're set) versus double opt-in (enter address, confirm in an e-mail) versus triple[82] (enter e-mail, plus Captcha phrase to prove you're real, then prove your e-mail is real), just remember that the more you make people click, the less you get. If you hear the sound of me stretching, that's just me getting ready to fight the group that says, "I would rather have 500 double opt-in subscribers than 2,000 single, because they are motivated!" Which is fine in theory; however, with confirmation rates averaging below 50 percent in many industries, that's a lot of people you're leaving out who initially raised their hand. Why not just try to

---

[82] There is one large newsletter service that makes you submit your e-mail, go to a secondary page, submit it again, check off interest boxes, and then gives you the option to give more personal info. Then you have to confirm via e-mail. Ta-da! Congrats! Your list has two people.

re-opt them in weekly! You may only have three subscribers, but damn they're motivated![83]

Your goal should be simple: Give people enough value on your site that they want to stay in touch and learn even more. Get them onto your value-driven list, make it easy for them to do so, and deliver them great content.

---

[83] They are also stalkers.

25

Captchas

ALLOWING PEOPLE TO take the next step with you through your website—be that a newsletter sign-up or a contact form submission—is exactly what you are aiming for at the end of the day. Creating barriers within that process can only hurt you. One of the biggest barriers are misguided Captcha forms. You may not have heard of the term, but I am sure you have seen these forms. Captcha is that box that asks you to type in the "words" you see in a box to confirm that you are an actual human being.

I understand the purpose of the Captcha, which is to stop spam robots.[84] And if you have ever been a victim of one of these spambots hitting your site, the onslaught of spam submissions is practically unbearable. However, shifting the onus of proof to the potential subscriber or client can cause you to frustrate and possibly lose that person. I am not stubborn enough to think that people pound the keyboard and in fits of rage refuse to fill out the word "duck" that they see in a box. The problem with using Captchas to verify if someone is human, as opposed to an automated program, is

---

[84] Picture illiterate terminators made out of canned ham. John Connor would be proud.

Figure 25.1 Captcha Box

that they're too hard to read and end up frustrating your potential user/customer. Recently I tried to sign up for a premium membership to a video-hosting site and was presented with this at checkout. See Figure 25.1.[85]

I actually have better than 20/20 vision. I have a somewhat strong command of the English language and did really well on my grade three test about letters, shapes, and sizes, but I could not tell you what that second word is if you offered to pay me a million dollars. It looks like a poorly drawn bat, one that you would sketch out with your friend on a napkin in a bar to visualize the plot of *Batman Returns*—but there was not enough room to type that.[86]

The result of this bat Captcha is that the company lost the sale. I tried to refresh the Captcha three more times and the same hilarity ensued. If you use Captcha on your site, test it out once in awhile to see if you can actually read it. It may be one of the reasons why you are not getting the number of submissions you want.

Pop-Ups

Back in the 1990s (or the Stone Age in Internet years), somebody got the brilliant idea to create a pop-up page—sort of like a virtual jack-in-the-box, except you weren't expecting it, nor did you ask for it. A virtual kick in the face to say *Hey! Look at me!*—like the

---

[85] Captcha generated by FeedBurner.com.

[86] I tried once to describe the movie *Goonies* to someone at a bar by using a napkin. I looked at it the next day and all I could see was two stick figures, a chocolate bar, and something that resembled a unicorn. There is no unicorn in *Goonies*.

child who did not get enough attention from his parents—the pop-up was eventually scorned and sent away to its room. Browsers were installed with pop-up blockers and banned from many sites.

Fast-forward to the present day and there is a new breed of pop-up ads, ones that hover over the page.[87] This is what amazes me about business and human beings in general. People fight to get rid of an annoyance and business fights to get around them to continue to annoy them. The thing about pop-ups is that they are fairly effective at building a list, but when you kick your market in the face with one, you are not considering how many people you turned away with them. The pop-up is almost created out of a fear that people will leave your site without signing up for your newsletter. But you should really be focusing on creating valuable and compelling content with an easy option for people to receive more. That could be a well-highlighted subscribe box on the right side of your blog or a postscript (P.S.) at the bottom of a great post reminding people that if they want to continue to receive this great content, all they have to do is fill out the form beside the post.

---

[87] I actually had someone argue with me once that what he was using was a hover and not a pop-up. I don't care if it is doing the salsa across my screen, it is a pop-up!

26

Experience Gap

ONE OF THE things companies need to realize is that they are only as good as the weakest experience of their customer. Many businesses are guilty of creating a great experience to get a first sale from you, but then they are really bad at keeping that level of service going. Once these customers get to the post–first-sale place, their experiences change. Your service is only as good as the worst experience a customer will have, not the best. It works with that age-old phrase: You are only as strong as your weakest link.

The space between the best services, often what a new customer receives, and the worst experience is what I call the Experience Gap. As a business owner your goal needs to be having no gap at all, optimizing every point of contact with your customer. As the gap grows, so will your customer's dissatisfaction.

I recently experienced this gap myself on two different occasions. The first was a negative experience with a store where I had shopped for a long time—Future Shop. The second was an outstanding experience with Cirque du Soleil in Las Vegas.

I was shopping for a voice-to-text software program that allows me to dictate into the computer and have it translated into text—one of the important tools that I am using to write this book. My amazing Twitter followers recommended a particular brand, and I found the title at Best Buy, one of my favorite electronic superstores. The title was on sale and therefore sold out there, so I decided to take the trip across the street to a competing retailer, Future Shop.

One of the things that both of these stores offer their customers is price matching—meaning that they will match a competitor's pricing. I was not a new customer to Future Shop, having bought multiple high-ticket items from them in the past. I went in and found the software I was looking for. Unlike Best Buy, they didn't have it on sale, so I grabbed a copy, found a sales associate, and requested that they price-match the $49 instead of its sticker price of $119.

The associate did not look impressed by my suggestion at all. I would describe the reaction more like one of contempt and frustration. Apparently, making my request for price-matching was going to be quite a chore. She went as far as to tell me that she would have to call Best Buy to see if they had any in stock, because that was the only way they would be willing to price-match. Even though I explained that it was only because Best Buy was sold out that I was even in her store, she spent 15 minutes finding a Best Buy location with the software on its shelves. So, finally she agreed to do the price-match and scanned the software into the computer. Turns out they had the software on sale as well, but no one had bothered to change the sticker price.

She did so many things wrong. It wasn't the fact that she had to follow company policy that was frustrating to me. I understand why these policies are in place, having worked in retail for a long time. I know the game. It was her attitude that changed my experience. People need to know this.

Just like the story I related in the beginning of this book, a single person can affect a customer's experience—this can happen for the good, as was the case with Wes at the Wynn, or for the bad. Now please understand this wasn't even a really big deal; the sales rep at Future Shop didn't yell at me or throw something at me. It wasn't like some of those outrageous stories I have heard, or seen, or even experienced myself in stores. But it is a really good example of a place not backing up what they claim to offer customers in a real day-to-day experience. In the end the store matched the price, but part of being a satisfied customer is being happy with the experience as well, not just the result.

I could probably write an entire book, as I am sure could you, just talking about the day-to-day experience of customers. The sad realization is that average customer service is actually below average. Unfortunately, most of the time you feel like a king for just getting your expectations met! When the bar is set so low, there really should be no excuse for any company not to exceed customer expectations.

27

Raising and Keeping the Bar High—Cirque

AN EXAMPLE OF a company that raised the bar for me and kept it that high is Cirque du Soleil. I first saw them in Las Vegas. The show was "Ka" at the MGM Grand. I had no expectation other than that I was told it was going to be a great show.

From the second I got to the door, my experience began. Everyone was in character—from the person who scanned my ticket at the door all the way to the bartender.[88] They all really cared about what they were saying. The bartender didn't shrug his shoulders and halfheartedly list off the drink options. Instead, he said this is the beer I suggest and this is why I like it. It was like when you ask a server in a restaurant what they suggest you order from the menu.

When we entered the theater to see the show, the usher who led us to our seats was so happy to see us and also in character. The way he sat us down really set the tone—he was so funny. The most amazing thing about all of this care and attention to the entire experience was that Cirque du Soleil didn't even need to do these things because the show itself is so incredible. I would see it again

---

[88] He suggested I try Fat Tire.

and again just for the show. What sets Cirque even more apart is that the company really understood the experience gap concept. It does not want anything to take away from the experience, not even a rude usher or two or the bartender to hurt it.

What took it to the next level for me, even after seeing Cirque shows multiple times since then, was when I mentioned how much I love them on Twitter. To my surprise, an hour later the actual Cirque du Soleil account on Twitter replied back! Someone was listening and the person replied! The rep tweeted back about how proud he is of the show and how great it makes him feel when others feel the same way. This was my first experience with a company that monitored social media and used it to engage with people in this way.

I really recommend you go online and check out the Twitter account @Cirque.[89] You see a mixture of show announcements and customer service. The company replies to its customers about all kinds of things—from how to get tickets, questions about the shows, and to say thank you to fans. The company even replies to reviews that are not all positive, showing that someone is listening, and also that the company has a lot of confidence in what it does. Cirque uses its Twitter account to show how much it appreciates its customers' business. Jess Berlin, who runs the Cirque account on Twitter, is someone I have gotten to know since that time. I've learned that she really does care about people having a great experience with Cirque. You need people like this in your company. You need people who will not only engage with others, but who want to do so, because it shows.

I've now seen Ka four times in Vegas, paying the full price three of those times just so I could take friends or clients to show them the example of excellence—to show clients the lack of excellence gap in this amazing company. I even tested the company

---

[89] Twitter.com/cirque

when they came to Toronto. I took my mom for her birthday to one of Cirque's traveling shows. And just like in Vegas, the experience was consistently at the highest level. In Toronto, the ushers were not actors in costume, yet it felt like they had a genuine concern to make sure that I had the greatest experience I possibly could with my mom, and I did.

28

Stirring Coffee

IF YOU RUN an established business, then you know how many customers you have, but do you know if they are happy? It takes about 5 to 10 times the amount of work to bring in a new customer as it does to retain a current customer. When you know this, why do you spend so much time and attention focusing only on attracting new business? You need to be giving at least this much focus on satisfying your current customers. Satisfied customers are the best way to market your business, because they are the ones who become your word-of-mouth army—they are your customer evangelists.[90]

Yet we ignore them. Commercials, programs, and plans are almost all directed toward incentives for new customers. There are famous stories out there of people who ignore current customers. We make it hard for them to return things. We make them wait on phones for 20 minutes, ensuring them that their business is important to us, so please stay on just a little longer, while we focus on the new customer on the other line. We put out the red carpet

---

[90] This is a great term from a great book called *Creating Customer Evangelists* by Ben McConnell and Jackie Huba.

for new sales and drag our feet to provide good service to the ones we already have.

Remember the hierarchy of buying—who was at the top? A current satisfied customer. This is where you are at your highest level of trust and the strongest point of your relationship. Sadly, some companies let their customers fall off the top of the mountain.

I have a morning ritual that I know many of you share. Coffee around here is a bit like a religion. You choose your brand, you pick your favorite, and then you stick with it. In the Toronto area, Tim Hortons is the church of coffee. It is a part of the culture up here, part of the vocabulary. When you say you're going for coffee, you go to "Tim's" or you're going to go to "Hortons."

I'm sure you have your own coffee chains in your area that have the same kind of following. They become a part of our routine. This has to be the ultimate goal for a business, whether it is service- or product-based. You work to become a part of somebody's routine. If you can achieve this goal, it is worth an incredible amount of money. The lifetime value of every person who spends $2 a day with your company is incredible. Think about that for a second—$2 a day equals more than $700 a year. Over 10 years you're looking at more than $7,000 in revenue from one person. Companies have a vested interest in making sure you become a regular, and you should be working hard to make your lifelong clients out of your customers. Unfortunately, just like many personal relationships, when you become used to one another you take each other for granted, and companies do this far too often with their loyal customers.

Tim Hortons had me. I was loyal as could be. But recently I have done something I never thought I would do: I changed brands. Being a loyal Tim Hortons customer, almost every day I would get my coffee from them. I didn't even think about it—that is just what I did. When any other coffee company came into the area, they were an afterthought. No way a new company was going to change my habit. Slowly something happened. I started noticing cracks in the armor of my habit. One misstep or one small issue will not lead to somebody changing a day-to-day habit, but when you begin to add up enough of those small things, you open the door to your competition. It is not usually extreme customer service issues that drive people away.

So here is the story of the small things that led me away from Tim Hortons. First, the servers wouldn't stir my coffee. The coffee was inconsistent, a small thing, but one that I know my fellow coffee drinkers out there will understand. When you buy your coffee at the drive-through and start to drink it after you've pulled a mile or two away and find that it was not made or stirred properly, the experience is hurtful. For people like me who take three sugars in their coffee[91] and order the same coffee every day, I really do notice the difference when it isn't made properly. Similarly, when there are mistakes in the order, when I can taste cream instead of milk, when there is sweetener instead of sugar, customers will notice. These are little things. Mistakes happen, of course, but when they start happening more and more, customers begin to wonder if this is how service will always be. Then customers begin to doubt the quality of your service or product. This doubt creates a space where customers are open to trying something new.

Picture the image of a gap. It starts as a tiny crack. Your loyal customer has always been happy with your product or service, and then slowly small doubts add up and cracks begin to form—until one day, the experience gap grows just big enough for one of your competitors to get through. The experience gap is the space between the best experience your customer has had with you and the worst. Ideally this gap doesn't exist or is as small as possible.

Businesses need to make buying their products easy. This was another issue with Tim Hortons that led me away from being a

---

[91] Or, as my Grama used to say, boiled candy cream. She used to get mad at me for putting too much sugar in my coffee.

loyal customer. Until recently, the company did not accept debit card payments,[92] so many of their customers cannot pay for their coffee and doughnuts with a bankcard. This is rare today. As a matter of fact, the only reason I would ever take money out of the bank was so I could buy coffee from Hortons.

Now the extra inconvenience of taking out cash was okay when my coffee was perfect, but adding this to the frequency of mistakes in my order was getting to be too much. Add in some other things I put up with in the name of my favorite coffee, such as the cumbersome lid that was impossible to open while driving, and the long wait times, and I was really open to the competition. I had been a loyal customer for 20 years. I figured that over that time I have spent upward of $15,000 with the company.

I was at that point where all of these small negative experiences had come together, the perfect storm point, and I was open to giving something else a try. It takes a lot for somebody to change anything, let alone a part of their daily routine. I didn't really do it consciously, it just happened. All that it was going to take for another company to earn me as a new customer was quality that matched what I was used to and that gave me more convenience.

Enter McDonald's. I was already a McDonald's fan. The company didn't have to begin at the start with me or get me to buy into its brand. But I didn't buy coffee there. My first real job was working at McDonald's when I was 15. As far as I could see back then, the only people who bought coffee at McDonald's were senior citizens at 6 AM. But now McDonald's was on a mission to prove that its coffee was worth buying on its own, a bold task considering the market already included heavy competition from Hortons and Starbucks.

---

[92] Since the hardcover of this book came out, most locations now accept debit cards. You're welcome.

A few years ago I wouldn't have even thought of trying the McDonald's coffee, let alone switching over to it, but I had gotten to the breaking point as a customer. I was willing to at least try something different. Tim Hortons was taking my business for granted, but McDonald's was working for it. McDonald's had a promotion to launch its coffee, and it was giving out free coffee during a certain time, so this was going to be the time I would try it. Unfortunately the lineup of people to try the coffee when they found out it was free could have rivaled lineups for rides at Disney World, so I decided to hold off on giving it a try. A few weeks later I finally went in and tried it.

Compared with Tim Hortons, McDonald's had the same, if not more, drive-through locations, just the kind of convenience a lazy man like myself was looking for. At this point the quality was important—no matter how much convenience or customer service I got, at this point if the product wasn't of the quality that I liked, I wouldn't switch to it. This is really important to note: Quality is always important! No matter how much marketing or UnMarketing you do, it doesn't make a difference if your product or service doesn't stand up. So I order the coffee and go to pay for it and the server takes my bankcard! I am allowed to use my bankcard to pay for the coffee—McDonald's earned one bonus point.

I get the coffee and I see that the coffee cup is double-walled, meaning I don't have to put a sleeve on it! I don't have to ask for a second cup! McDonald's execs have spent some time thinking about their products and their customers and thought, "Hey, coffee is hot, people don't like to burn their hands," and come up with a solution—a double-walled cup. Genius. I went to open the cup in my car, and the lid was amazing. You can open it with one thumb, and it pops and locks open—no mess, no burned fingers, and another bonus point. The ease and convenience of the cup itself really improved my experience.

The McDonald's location near my home also has a secret weapon. His name is David. At the Iroqouis Shore Road location, in Oakville, Ontario, David is the guy you talk to in the morning in the drive-through. He's kind, considerate, and happy, but not the "in-your-face kind of happy" that makes you hate him in the morning. Heck, he even makes the add-on suggestion of a muffin a pleasant occurrence. It's gotten to the point that I will go out of my way in the morning to have David serve me. So I found great service and a great new product. I never would've even known if it hadn't been for the "dropping of the ball" from the place where I was loyal.

This is exactly what your company does not want. You do not want your longtime loyal customer to be dissatisfied too many times and now in the hands of the competition and very, very happy. I then tasted the coffee and it was great. I get no reimbursement from McDonald's to say that I am not their affiliate. In all honesty, the coffee tasted great, even better than what I was used to. That did it. And now I look for McDonald's when I'm wanting a morning coffee or on the road. I may be just one customer, but my lifetime value is $20,000 or $30,000. How many people will it take for Tim Hortons to realize that understanding the needs and wants of the marketplace is important all the time?

You need to know if your customers are happy, and if they aren't you need to know why and how you can change it. You need to know where you stand in the eyes of your customers. Are they happy, are they ecstatic, or are they just there holding on until someone better comes along? You do not want your brand to be in that zone with current customers where the experience gap has left a space for the competition. You cannot be complacent or inattentive, leaving your hard-earned market ripe for the picking.

Now, because you are reading this book, you are ready to think differently about how you treat your customers. You know that every point of contact is an opportunity to engage with your market—this is true for your current customers as well. If you want to find out where you stand with your customers, finding out is simple: ask them.

Some retail operations are doing this successfully right now. As an example, Future Shop is currently inviting customers to participate in an online survey at the bottom of their receipts. The company gives customers an incentive to participate by giving those who complete the survey the chance to win a gift card. Now, it will lose some people because there is a transfer of mediums, where the customer has to make the effort to go online. Future Shop addresses this by giving the gift incentive, and I think this shows really well that the company appreciates its customers' time. Still, the participation rate will be lower than if the customer was already shopping online. Another way to engage your customers is by e-mail.

A simple thing you can do is what I call "Stop Start Continue." Use an online survey service, Survey Monkey, for example. You can send out a brief e-mail to your customer list. Ask customers these three simple questions: (1) "What should we stop doing?" (2) "What should we start doing?" and (3) "What do you think we should continue doing to ensure we not only meet but exceed your expectations?" Business owners incorrectly think that their customers will say something if they are unhappy. But most people will not say anything at all; they just stop buying. The time to ask customers what you can do to improve their experience is not when they are angry and/or have already gone elsewhere, but when they are currently customers with you. How many times have you gotten an e-mail from a place where you are a current client asking you to tell the company what it can do to serve you better? I know it has not happened often to me, and I know that the feedback you get will surprise you.

29

Experience Gap for Small Biz

THE EXPERIENCE GAP concept applies to small companies, too, even one-person operations. An experience can be anything—it does not have to be transactional. The experience can be any point of engagement, or even someone simply noticing something about your business. That's one of the things business owners need to be cautious of when using social media.

I love the fact that with social media I get to know business owners. I can learn not just about their businesses but also about them personally. Sharing this type of connection builds greater trust than any brochure, logo, or company mission statement could. But making a personal connection means that you also have to be careful what you put out there.

You see it happen on Twitter all the time, especially when people start talking about sensitive topics like politics or religion. A few months ago there was a huge protest in Toronto. A group was trying to bring attention to what it believed was our country's lack of involvement in what it viewed as a great injustice on the people of another country. I watched and observed closely, not to see people's opinions on the issue but to see what kind of opinions were coming out under company accounts. A "company account" is one that you run for your business. You see, sadly, many comments on Twitter that could be considered racist, ignorant, and bigoted—not exactly the things you want related to your company.

The problem is that many sites, especially ones like Twitter, are reaction-based. They are emotionally driven. And in the height of emotional issues, you often need to step back for a moment and think. Never put something on a social media site (or anywhere online) that you do not want seen on a billboard with your name, your picture, your company logo, and your phone number on it, with your mom driving by while sitting shotgun. Even if you delete something on the Web, the Internet never forgets.

As I mention all the time, I see many men writing things casually on Facebook and Twitter that make me feel greasy, whether they are inappropriate comments about a picture or general statements that they think somebody wants to hear. Again, if you want a billboard with your company's name on it and you're saying the line "love your new sweet haircut hot stuff, would love to get me some of that," then by all means, Casanova, go for it.

Sometimes negative experiences are not our fault. Let's call this the involuntary experience gap. Perfect examples of this are phishing scams or being a victim to a virus and spreading it around to your friends and followers without knowing it. It's happened to all of us.

The problem is that now it is just so easy to spread certain things along social media channels. Scammers take advantage of this by sending something falsely in "your name." People who trust you will open these messages without thinking twice and then keep the scam going. In a phishing scam your account is taken over after you fill out your name and password on a phishing site. It looks like you're logging into a trusted site, but in reality it's a fake to grab your log-in information.

I have found that people are usually forgiving about this kind of thing as long as it only happens once. But right or wrong, your fault or not, it is still a reflection of your company and part of your market's experience with you. That is why it is so important to educate yourself and anyone who uses your social media accounts about phishing scams and viruses and how they can be spread and prevented.

30

Using Stop Start Continue

I HAD A client a while back, a private school in the Toronto area. One of its biggest issues was reenrollment. When parents decided not to send their children back the following school year, the school found out too late to deal with the issue(s) and possibly keep the student. Together, we implemented a survey system to test customer satisfaction. We e-mailed 120 families with children currently enrolled in the school. We started the conversation, engaged with the parents, and got them talking about their experience. We allowed them to choose to answer anonymously or to leave out their contact information.

Going back to the trust gap, we had already achieved the highest level of trust we could, because these parents trusted us with the well-being of their children. This makes it even more important for the experience gap to be nearly nonexistent. In a relationship with a high level of trust, you cannot afford gaps in either trust or experience, because you cannot usually gain it back once you have lost it.

Using an online service for the survey allowed us to create a quick database of all the results. The e-mail was sent out, and we had a 95 percent response rate. Within 48 hours we sat down with the head of the school and the faculty with 45 pages of collected results—all feedback from current parents. Some of the information was pretty basic, like wanting more variety on the lunch menu. Some pointed to more serious issues for the children. There was also a lot of positive feedback, with stories of happy customers. The positive feedback is great for so many reasons. You can learn what's working and also drum up testimonials for your business, which is always great for attracting new customers.

This is where you have the opportunity for engagement. You've got your clients' attention, you have their ears, now you need to follow up. Just hearing what they have to tell you is the first step, but it can't be the last. You may not change anything based on something one of your customers told you, but if you see something consistently coming up that you are not delivering, then you know you need to act.

After going through all the feedback from the school survey, we sat around a boardroom table and every single response was delegated to somebody to take responsibility for. We made sure that every person who had participated in the study was validated and knew that they had been heard. We also made sure that the participants were thanked for their time and knew that whatever the concern, the school was working hard to improve the quality of their service. By the following week, the school had followed up with every single parent.

Try sending these questions out to your list, whether they are customers or subscribers to your newsletter. The parents of students at the private school did not need any extra incentive for filling out the survey because they were investing a lot of money in the school and the service had a lot of value. But in other kinds of circumstances, such as if you're asking free subscribers of your newsletter about something, you may want to throw in a gift to thank them for their time. You can add an Amazon.com gift card or something that you can raffle off for people as a thank you. I did this with a list of mine and got 10,000 responses.[93]

You can ask your list members what type of content they want to read. You could ask them what delivery methods they like for products. But most importantly, start by asking your current customers the "Stop Start Continue" questions. These questions will improve your business, keep you moving forward, and save you from losing customers. This engagement will enhance your relationship with satisfied customers.

---

[93] It astounds me what people will do to try and get something for free. I see this in Vegas all the time—people spend $200 to earn a free buffet coupon. Do they know the buffet is actually $10?

31

Zappos

UNMARKETING IS ALL about engagement at every point of contact with your market. If you believe that every employee in your company has a role in marketing, then you have to look at how they engage with your customers on a day-to-day basis. As an example of how to do this right, you don't have to look any further than Zappos.com. This company empowers every member of its team to create an environment where each employee has the ability to really put the customer's needs first.

There are a few things that I have personally noticed that make Zappos.com stand out. Most importantly, the company has a brand based on excellent customer service. If you asked someone to define Zappos.com in one word, he or she will not say "shoes" or even "online store" but will say "service." How many of you reading this chapter now can say that about your company? That your company's quality of service is so good, so well known, that service is actually what you're known for?

One of the ways that Zappos.com made this happen is by having a generous return policy. The company started out by selling shoes as an online vendor. It faced a huge hurdle going against classic shoe stores to earn its customers. Buyers were used to trying on shoes. Zappos.com had to bridge the trust gap and convince customers that they could buy shoes online, without trying them on. What was the first question people had for them? "If they don't fit, can I return or exchange them?" Zappos.com said "yes" and earned the trust of their market. The Zappos.com website states on its return pages that, "If you are not 100 percent satisfied, you can return your item(s) for a full refund within 365 days of purchase."

But Zappos.com's branding is not just about the free shipping and a long grace period for returns. The stories of its efforts to gain satisfied customers are everywhere online. One story that gives me chills is about a person who had ordered multiple pairs of shoes for his mother. She sadly took ill and was in the hospital. Not knowing what exact size of shoe would fit his mother or exactly what she may like, he decided to order nine different pairs of shoes to have her try them on and then return the ones that either didn't fit or she didn't want. Sadly, his mother passed away, and later on he realized he had never returned any of the pairs of shoes that he ordered. They added up to a substantial amount of money. He sent an e-mail to Zappos.com explaining his situation, wondering if there was anything that they could do for him so that he could return all of the shoes. No one had ever worn them, and there were so many pairs. He understood that he was outside of the return window, but he thought he would give it a try and contact the company.

The customer service representative who received the e-mail let him know right away, that day in fact, that the company would arrange for a UPS truck to show up at his house the following day to pick up all the boxes. His credit card would be credited the full amount of the original purchase, and he would not be charged for the return shipping. The representative also expressed the company's condolences on the loss of his mother. When the delivery truck arrived the next day to collect the shoes, the driver also brought along a bouquet of flowers with deepest sympathies from the customer service representative who had spoken to him the day before.

The customer was overwhelmed by this response. Wouldn't you be? When was the last time you received service like this from a company? He then blogged about it, and that blog has been viewed by thousands of people. The thing is, Zappos.com did not perform its service with the goal of this customer's blogging about it; the company does not do things so that people will tweet about them. Zappos.com truly believes that every experience a customer or potential customer has is a chance to wow them. The company cares about its customers, and this is what defines the Zappos.com brand and separates this company from the crowd.

You know what else is amazing about Zappos.com? The tour! If you have a chance to go to their facility in Nevada, you have to do it. It is an amazing experience! I saw this firsthand when I accepted the company's offer of a tour of its facilities in Las Vegas. Anyone can do it. A company rep will pick you up in a shuttle from any-where in the area and drop you off anywhere else in Vegas you want to go after the tour, free of charge.

I wanted to see what all the hoopla was about, having heard about the tour from other people, and to see if there was an experi-ence gap even on a tour with the company. I wanted to know if there was a difference between what I would experience and all of the amazing stories I had heard or read online. The problem with setting great examples that circulate online is that you set great expectations. When you earn a reputation for greatness, people come to expect that from you going forward.

This tour even exceeded my already high expectations. From the woman who drove the shuttle bus, who had moved from Ken-tucky just to work for Zappos.com, to every stop on the tour, I was engaged and impressed. I left with better faith in humankind that companies can run at a high level. The tour started with our tour guide, one of the top people in management, holding a large flag. The flag let everyone know, as we walked through the offices, that we were esteemed guests of a tour.

The hilarious part is that when you take the tour, every time you pass a group of cubicles or a team, they have their own thing they do for the tour. The first group we passed stopped what they were doing, opened their desk drawers, and each of them grabbed a camera and started taking pictures of us, cheering the entire time. Another group had those party clappers and waved them loudly at us. Another team had a song for us. Not one person looked put off or as if they were forced into this. Now, I am sure that every now and again when someone is having a bad day their team whipping into a verse of "It's a Small World After All" isn't the best thing for a headache, but still. I spent years in human resources and consulting, going into work places and speaking with employees. I know unhappy workers; I can feel them. I know the look. The employees I saw and met that day at Zappos.com were happy to work there. They were valued parts of the team and enjoyed their work. We should all run companies like that.

When we arrived at the call center part of the tour, I noticed the lack of a call-board. This is a popular piece in any call center that ranks each person on his or her call times. Most call centers judge their workers by how quickly they can get somebody off the phone. I noticed that the call-board was missing and asked the tour guide where it was. He actually laughed at the question. Zappos.com does not use a call-board. Call center reps have no set limit of time to talk to their customers. The shortest call that they had recorded was 40 seconds and the longest call was four hours.

The tour guide also added that the woman who was on the four-hour call did not end up buying a single thing. At Zappos.com the call center representative had a simple job—to help people. The reps were not on the phone with customers only to pick something out so they could buy it. They were there to help them.

To let customers know about products that they were buying online that they couldn't touch. They just blew me away. Do you know that Zappos.com allows their phone representatives to source a product for a customer even if they don't carry it and it is from one of their competitors? They are empowered to send the customer in whatever direction is needed to help them. The reps have that much confidence in service. They understand that giving the customer a good experience will be remembered and is valuable. They believe this so much that they came up with their 10 core values, as follows taken from their website:

> As we grow as a company, it has become more and more important to explicitly define the Zappos core values from which we develop our culture, our brand, and our business strategies. These are the 10 core values that we live by:
>
> 1. Deliver WOW Through Service
> 2. Embrace and Drive Change
> 3. Create Fun and a Little Weirdness
> 4. Be Adventurous, Creative, and Open-Minded
> 5. Pursue Growth and Learning
> 6. Build Open and Honest Relationships with Communication
> 7. Build a Positive Team and Family Spirit
> 8. Do More with Less
> 9. Be Passionate and Determined
> 10. Be Humble

You can't really argue with any of those 10 points. One of the biggest drivers behind this culture is CEO Tony Hsieh. It would be very difficult to drive a culture like this without it being from the top down. He is @Zappos on Twitter.

32

Rockport

AS YOU READ in the opening of the book, one person's attitude can change the perception of a brand. This can also be done with products, like what happened with Rockport shoes and me last year. I was tweeting away, mentioning my upcoming Vegas trip and reminding myself out loud to buy some new shoes because I had made the moronic error of wandering the Vegas strip in flip-flops on my last trip.[94]

Somebody replied to me that he had the perfect shoes for me and would "hook me up." I thought this was just another person talking big online about his or her connections and what he could do for people. He later sent me a DM mentioning that he would send me what he wears because he does a lot of walking. This is where the relationships online can get a wee bit weird. I had to wonder if this guy was about to send me a pair of his used sandals. However, my desire for free stuff trumped my concern for hygiene. I said, "Ah, what the hell, why not?" and sent him my home address and shoe size. He replied saying he was going away for a few weeks and would

---

[94] If you have never been to Vegas, that experience is like walking a marathon on the surface of the sun. Flip-flops don't cut it.

take care of it when he got home. Besides the fact that I just gave my address out to a total stranger, not to mention my shoe size, I was feeling quite good about it. I then proceeded to forget all about it.

A few weeks later, the buzzer went off at my condo, and it was a delivery guy. Thankfully not the guy I was talking to online. He was dropping off a huge box. I opened the box and there were three boxes inside, all from Rockport. Understand that up to that very moment Rockport shoes to me represented shoes for old people and those with foot problems—and then I opened the boxes. Inside was a pair of wicked, classy, running-style shoes, a pair of fancy loafers, and a pair of black leather boots with buckles on them that may have well said "badass" on them—they were that good! Instantly, not only did my view of the Rockport brand change, but I fell in love with them.

However, now I had to reply to this guy who I then discovered was one of the designers for Rockport. Since this was my first bribe, I sent him a DM to thank him and to ask what I should do next. Was I supposed to blog about it, or tweet about them? There was no letter in the box requesting that I review them. He replied, "Just enjoy the shoes," and that's it. ☺ He just pulled some triple reverse mind screw on me. I knew he wanted me to talk about the shoes. He knew he wanted me to talk about the shoes. I wanted to talk about the shoes. Well played, sir. What do you think I did next? I talked about the shoes to anybody who would listen. I wear them in presentations. I talk about them in presentations. I even runway model them in presentations. And look what happened here, I even talked about them in my book. Well played again, Rockport mind ninja, well played.

I am not saying to just send out free products to everybody on Twitter.[95] I know I was sent the shoes because even at that time I

---

[95] Just to me. I am fully open to bribes. And to be honest, after writing 64,000+ words, I'm spent, I've got nothing left. Imagine how many words I could use to describe your sending me a car, a boat, or a vacation home.

had a good presence, I had a big mouth, and he was a nice guy and thought he would help out. The cool thing about him was the fact that he didn't even mention Rockport in his profile. He is there for his own personal account and thought it would be fun to help out. But it shows what happens if you have confidence in your product and can send it out to the right people.

33

FreshBooks

"We wouldn't do it if it didn't make business sense."

That statement defined customer engagement for me. It was spoken by Mike McDerment, CEO of FreshBooks, an online invoicing, time-tracking, and expense service. I was on a marketing panel with him last year, and I was spewing my normal sermon about how you need to build relationships, when he interrupted me with that statement. I loved it. Meaning at the end of the day, as a business you have to justify financially your engagement efforts. FreshBooks is not only able to see that it helped their bottom line, but the execs are experts at it.

In 2008, FreshBooks company reps famously drove an RV from the Future of Web Apps conference in Miami, Florida, all the way to South by Southwest in Austin, Texas. They made this trip, in this way, so that they could meet as many of their users during the trip as possible and spread the word about their company. They stopped along the way and took people out for dinner. They made videos during the entire trip and uploaded them to YouTube.

But it's not the big public things that FreshBooks reps do that makes me want to sing their praises—it's the individual efforts that make them stand out. For example:

- Michelle Wolverton, a virtual assistant based out of Boston, tweeted about being stood up on a date. FreshBooks reps responded, "We'd never stand you up." That's already pretty sweet—kind of unexpected coming from a brand. But, the next day, they sent her flowers—something not terribly common coming from a web app you pay a monthly bill for—and made a friend for life. Michelle still screams her love of them from the rooftop, and they'd still never stand her up![96]

- A while ago, Mike McDerment wrote a blog post mentioning some new flavors of Triscuits. Jonathon, a customer of theirs, commented on the blog post, joking that they shouldn't talk about things he can't pick up in his home in Fiji. The Fresh-Books team felt for Jonathon, so they took the liberty of sending him a couple boxes of Triscuits. He was excited when he received them. So excited, in fact, that he wrote a feature article in the *Fiji Times* titled "Separating the Good Buzz from the Bad" about FreshBooks and a handful of other businesses with outstanding service that had touched him.[97]

Even the new-hire process at FreshBooks focuses on support. McDerment told me:

Everyone who starts at FreshBooks—no matter their role, marketing, VP, CEO—starts by doing customer support for at least two months. There's no better way to get to know the product and our customers than talking to them and answering questions. Four days a week, a new hire's job is to pick up the phone, answer e-mail, and respond to forum posts.

When someone graduates from support, he or she is still responsible for one day on support about once every three weeks or so. We have a core support team every day built up of our support team and members of other teams assigned to do support for the day. All their other tasks are put on hold until the next day.[98]

FreshBooks is active on Twitter @freshbooks as well, both with personality and support for customers, all out in the open. So, as Mike said, treating your customers well is good for business.

---

[98] http://bit.ly/68pKZa, to see its new-hire blog.

34

Why You Can't Learn From Millionaires

YOU CAN ADMIRE and take points from someone, but you shouldn't try to be that person or company. You don't see behind the curtain. The crib notes of the company's success don't show the other 99.99 percent of the things it did to get to the place it is at today. Frankly, I can't learn much from someone who made millions years ago and is running that business today. The tools are different, as is that person's leverage. You can take tips and inspiration, but managers' opinions may not be as practical with today's tools. What worked in the 1980s may not work today.[99] There are better, more efficient, cheaper ways to get in front of your marketplace today than ever before.

As an example, a friend of mine told me about a speaker at a recent conference she had attended. She made a gabillion dollars.[100] She got on stage in front of hundreds of business owners and stated that the audience was wasting its time using social media and being on Facebook and Twitter. She said the audience was

---

[99] Insert crack at the Yellow Pages and cold calling here.

[100] I rounded up. Give or take a gabillion.

better off focusing on the branding practices of Coke and the other Fortune 50 companies. My friend said that you could see the look of panic on the attendees' faces. The people who had been building real relationships online to help their businesses grow were now being told they were doing it all wrong by someone they aimed to be like. The speaker also admitted that she got to where she was today by lying to a buyer of one of the store chains to get her product placed. Oh, and the conference theme? Being your true self. Well done.

The problem with trying to emulate a millionaire is that it isn't a business. Making money isn't a career. It's the result of good business. There is a huge difference between a result and the cause of the result. You can fall into the trap of simply wanting to be rich, and the next thing you know, you're sitting in a hotel conference room at a "free" seminar being told that the only way to get rich is to pay someone money to show you how to get rich. The smart cookies reading this will realize that the way the seminar leaders make money is by selling the programs on how to make money! Send me $5 in the mail right now, and I'll send you step-by-step instructions on how to make a million dollars, $5 at a time![101]

There will always be people who tell you that what you're doing is wrong, as well as those who will tell you that everything you're doing is right. Both should be avoided. Seek out the opinions of people you trust who can give encouragement but also honest feedback. Now is not the time to ask your mom if your website looks effective.[102] One of the best ways to find those people in business is through, you guessed it, social media. By building trusting relationships with people, you have at your disposal a potentially large group of experts who can give you feedback when you

---

[101] Please don't mail me $5. I'm sure it's breaking some federal law, and I won't send it back if you do. Consider it a cheap education on how to get scammed. You're welcome.

[102] Unless your mom is someone who understands websites and business, then by all means, ask! And send me her e-mail address—I want her to look at my site.

need it the most.[103] I believe in positive thinking and goal setting, but being oblivious is a surefire recipe for failure. You can read *The Secret* all you want, but business doesn't manifest itself. I saw an ad agency owner once credit the success of landing a large campaign to "manifesting it." What a great way to insult his entire team, which spent countless weeks, even months, to get it together. I'm sure the team was manifesting a thank you for him.

---

[103] Although I've learned, being a person who gives honest feedback, that people don't usually want it; they just want praise. That doesn't help anyone if it isn't true. Encouraging someone going down the wrong path hurts that person.

35

Transparency and Authenticity

THE TERMS TRANSPARENCY and *authenticity* have become quite the buzz terms lately. There are so many courses and workshops available out there that claim to teach you how to be your authentic self. The level of irony this speaks to is so high that I really don't know where to start with it. You do not need a consultant to teach you how to be yourself. Issues and challenges often do arise when you set out to decide where to draw the line with being yourself online and in business. You need to understand the difference between authenticity and transparency.

Authenticity in business is all about realizing that your strongest asset in your company should be you. When you stop trying to pretend to be like other people and focus on your own strengths, you bring authenticity to the table. Outsource your weaknesses and the things that you don't like to do, and remember your strengths. Your competition cannot be you.

Authenticity is easier. It is so much simpler just to be yourself. You never have to worry about remembering what you said about something to make sure you aren't contradicting yourself. Some people call being authentic "personal branding," but I just call it good business.

So where do you draw the line at being authentic? What is too much information or opinion to give out when it comes to your personal thoughts and life? This is a really important question to think about when you are using social media to promote your business or connect with your market. It relates to an experience I had a few weeks ago. Somebody with whom I have built a relationship at conferences and in social media retweeted a link that somebody had sent out opposing gay marriage. Everyone is entitled to his or her own views and opinions, but you need to understand that if you choose to be authentic you have to be prepared for the results.

Even though I have a business relationship with this person, it is still a relationship. Their views are not ones that I personally share, and that way of thinking is not something with which I want to be associated. Even if you are not the person who originally sent out a message or video, you are embracing and endorsing it by sending it out to your followers on Twitter. Besides, I don't really care about religion or politics; this is the real reason that I never discuss either anywhere. People will even argue with me about being agnostic, both religiously and politically. Don't reveal something for the sake of authenticity that you don't want to see on a billboard with your name, your face, your phone number, and your company logo on it.

Transparency in business and marketing really means being honest. In terms of transparency, sadly most people look to the FTC for guidelines (be sure to check what I've written previously on this topic). Transparency comes into play in all areas of business, including social media, events, testimonials, and even best-selling books.

One of the biggest issues in the debate around transparency is that it can be so subjective. It is defined by personal perspectives and our own value system. When you are faced with situations that call ethics into play, you have to do what you think is right. Just remember that other people, including your market, may have a higher standard than you, because perception is everything.

36

My Transparency on Twitter

WHEN I FIRST started getting some momentum on Twitter, gaining up to 500 new followers a day during the craziest of my tweeting addiction, I turned off notifications of new followers. I just could not keep up with them all. I then had a choice: become a Twitter Diva (or "Twiva" if you want to annoy the eggnog out of people) and not follow anyone back, or auto-follow everyone back who followed me. I picked the latter, because I figured it was a nice way to say thanks for following me, and hey, if they followed me they at least have that going for them. ☺

This was a mistake for three reasons:

1. *I followed back spammers and porn accounts and other undesirables.* I have nothing against porn stars. I'm sure they wake up and put on their latex pants like the rest of us, but I had no desire to hear about the sequel to *Long Dong Silver* in my tweet stream. Your profile page shows a collection of people you've recently begun to follow. Some of those profile pictures do not reflect well on your brand, and why are you following @WhipsAndChainsForMen anyway?

137

2. *I ended up following 30,000 people.* I barely look at my "All Tweets" screen. I removed it from TweetDeck. There is so much noise that I've had to make custom groups called *rockstars* and *awesomesauce* to read the tweets of people that I learn from or I know. I should have stayed selective in choosing those I followed back. These days I only follow those I learn from or laugh from or who engage with me or people I find interesting. If you are looking for a tool to manage your followers, a great one is ReFollow.com. I can check off "Not Following" and down below check off "Users who have @ mentioned me" to see who have been engaging with me but I haven't followed back. And don't get me started on all the auto-DMs that opened up. Even after using SocialToo.com to block most of the DMs, if I get one more "it lets your Facebook friends find you on Twitter" DMs, I'm going to start getting all stabby.

3. *It was not being transparent.* I was trading authenticity for automation. Efficiency for transparency. People would tweet or DM me that they were flattered that I followed them back, and I winced every time. I couldn't tell them that it was automated.

Twitter is different from a newsletter. There is a much more personal connection on it. Just like auto-tweeting, which I'll go over in the next section, as soon as you throw automation into your relationships, they stop being authentic. Is it worth deceiving people for the sake of automation? Because that is the way that followers might see it. I realized a little too late, my answer is "no."

37

Your Transparency on Twitter

AUTO-TWEETING OR ABSENT tweeting is the ability to send tweets out without your having to do it manually. There are a variety of websites and services that allow you to ghost tweet. People who argue in favor of these tools say that it allows them to keep a presence in the social media area even though they might be too busy, sleeping, or even while on stage speaking. When I polled a bunch of my followers about their thoughts of people using automated tweets, the reaction was overwhelmingly negative. Twitter is unique. People feel that when they see a tweet from your account that you are actually the person writing it at that time. Not to mention that if you use a tweet system that is sent out when you're not there, what you're saying to your followers is that you're only on there to talk and not listen.

An example of this was when I saw a well-known speaker who I knew was on a cruise for a week with no Internet access tweeting out a pitch for his upcoming workshop. People saw the tweet and replied and asked him specific questions about the workshop because they were interested in potentially attending—and nothing happened. No reply came from him until five days later when he returned from the cruise. When people asked why it took him so long to reply, he said, "Sorry, I was on a cruise for a week without access," which then led to the logical follow-up question: "If you had no access, how did you tweet about your workshop in the first place?" You see what can happen here? If you want to build a presence in the social media platform, then you need to be present.

In addition to absent tweeting, some people also use their assistants to tweet on their behalf, pretending to be them. Although potentially efficient, this method again hurts the transparency and the authenticity of your account. Your followers think that they are speaking to you. People get really upset with this technique for a good reason. You cannot, for the sake of automation, outsource your relationship building. Of all the areas of business, this is really the number-one thing that a business owner should not be delegating to someone else. You wouldn't send your assistant to go have coffee with somebody and pretend to be you,[104] and you wouldn't hire an actor to go and play you at a networking event.[105]

Please understand that this is not an argument about efficiency. Most people, including myself, do not have an issue if multiple people tweet from the same account as long as it's disclosed in the bio. Guy Kawasaki created quite a stir when he admitted in an interview that his Twitter account was run by three other people as well as him. He then changed his bio afterward to disclose that other people also tweet from his account, although that seems to be gone now as well. You can run multiperson accounts and simply add the initials to the end of the tweets. This way the readers will know that what they are reading may not be written by the main person on the account. This allows for the efficiency of a multiperson account while still being transparent.

---

[104] Although, that would be awesome—to send somebody in your own clothes and disguised with a fake moustache and try to talk like you . . . so good.

[105] Although again, how awesome would that be? I'm going to hire De Niro to represent me at the next conference. UnDe Niro.

38

Affiliates

ANOTHER ISSUE WITH transparency, one that the FTC has recently caused a huge stir about, is affiliate links—using affiliates for your business and being an affiliate for someone else's business. There are many benefits to having and/or being an affiliate, but there are also pitfalls. An affiliate is somebody who acts as almost an independent sales rep for your product or service. Affiliates became popular online when websites started to use cookies. A cookie is something that is placed on your computer that recognizes who sent you there in the first place.

Here is how it works: A vendor or business owner sets up a form on the shopping cart of the website where you can sign up to become an affiliate. From the information on the form, a unique affiliate link for you is generated that allows you to send people to the page. In turn, when you promote that person's business, and send traffic to their site, the link logs the fact that you were the one who sent them there. This means that if a person buys something immediately or even in the future,[106] you get credit for the

---

[106] The cookie can be set for a defined period of time, for example, the next 30 days.

sale. You then make a commission that is preset by the vendor—from 5 percent up to 95 percent, depending on the industry. Digital products like ebooks or online courses can offer a higher affiliate percentage because they have no cost of delivery or hard cost of goods.

The transparency issue here is that most of the time an affiliate link is masked. This means that you can't tell that the person who gave you the link is making a percentage of the potential sale. So should you? The FTC says that you have to disclose on a blog if a link you display is an affiliate link. So it opens up the question—Do you need to reveal this?

If you are using affiliates to promote your products or services, are you going to insist that they disclose that relationship upfront as well? One of the hesitations from business owners to use affiliates is the potential lack of promotional control. Whatever your affiliates say and do is a reflection of your company, and many companies choose not to do it at all. I like using affiliates. Where else can you hire an unpaid sales force that only makes money when you do?

39

Testimonials

YOU CAN GO to any bookstore, any sales page on a website, and almost all sales material in general and see glowing testimonials from popular or celebrity-level people. What most people do not know is that many of these testimonials were written by people who have never actually tried or read or experienced the product they are talking about. Some testimonials are prewritten by the product owner and then signed off on by the person. And I think that the worst offense is that the person has been paid to write a testimonial.

It's like a little club, especially in business book writing, where people can whip off testimonials faster than they can read a book. There are some authors out there, well-known, best-selling ones, who have given so many testimonials that they would have to average three books an hour to have read the actual books for which they are singing praise.

What most people don't know is that it is actually a profit center for some people. Sure, they say, I'll give you a testimonial for your crappy book, but it'll cost you $500, and you have to write the copy for it. Now the FTC does have endorsement guidelines out there, but the FTC is so understaffed and overworked that 99 percent of the time it never catches violations. You're supposed to disclose the fact that you receive your product for free or have been paid to endorse something, whether it's on a website, a TV commercial, or even potentially a book cover.

There is nothing wrong with testimonials—they show that other people actually like your products. However, when you get like me and stop trusting them, you look at all of them with a jaded eye. I would much rather see a testimonial from an actual user. This kind of testimonial gives me hard numbers of what this product has done for other people. I get asked to give testimonials all the time for books, resources, and workshops, but I rarely have time to go through them, and I don't have the heart to tell people that I just don't like their product.

One of the newest trends at conferences is to get video testimonials of the attendees about what they thought about the conference. They are not looking for honest feedback and constructive criticism but rather for a collection of "wow" clips to help sell the next conference or the recording of that conference. The problem is when they force attendees to record it. I've had it happen a number of times. Someone from the conference will walk up with a camera and say, "Please say a few words about the conference." Kind of puts you in a bad spot, especially when you didn't like the event. So what can you do? I tell the person that I will either write something in an e-mail about my thoughts or actually be honest with the video reviewer and give a constructive criticism and maybe a compliment or two. Of course, for the one conference I criticized, the recorder cut out the criticism part and kept in the compliment totally out of context.

So for your business, get comments from real people, real clients, real satisfied customers. Be known as the person who doesn't use the industry mouthpiece. Stand out from your competition.

40

Best Sellers

THERE IS NO better way for an author to get clout than to have a best-selling book.[107] The term *best seller* makes you sound like kind of a big deal. It helps get you speaking engagements, consulting contracts, and not to mention sell more copies of the book. It's the publishing industry's version of social proof. When someone reads or hears that a book is a best seller, then that person believes that thousands of people have tested it out and validated that it's good, but in many cases that never happened.

I'm not going to get into the old way of getting around the best-selling system, which was made popular both in the publishing of books and music with mass quantities of the product bought by the publishing house or label themselves to hit the bestseller list, just to be returned after the period had ended.

What I want to cover is the new way to screw the system—let's call it fake best seller 2.0. Amazon has a huge amount of clout in the world today, and their best-seller list updates hourly if not

---

[107] If you are reading this book after it has become a best seller, please know I am exempt from any of the rant that I put in this chapter. Do as I rant, not as I do.

more frequently. One unruly author figured out that if he sold a small amount of books in a short amount of time, the book could temporarily hit a best-seller list on Amazon, and then the author could claim that the book is a best seller.

So then the avalanche started. Authors created best-seller programs where they focused on selling as many books as possible in as small a window as possible, rather than spending months focusing their promotion to hit the *New York Times* best-seller list.[108] The other trick was focusing on a sublist of the best-seller lists, not to get on the main best-seller list, but a subsection of a subsection. So an author would rank number eight on Amazon for the best-selling book on marketing to people with red hair on Wednesdays in New Hampshire, and because that book category has few books published in it, the book is then called a *best seller*. The author then goes out and hits the newsletter lists and the streets claiming that he or she is a best-selling author.

Then along came the consultants who, for a fee from $2,000 to $5,000 and more, would guarantee best-seller status if you pay them for it. What they don't tell you is that the majority of the time the book won't be on the Amazon main best-seller list but rather a deep sublist. So are the authors outright lying that their books are best sellers? Maybe not fully. But to use the term that means one thing and working the system to make it mean another is at the least inauthentic and at the worst manipulative. There is no denying that authors want to sell books; they want the recognition of best-seller status, including the guy who wrote this little book you're reading right now. But you won't see a best-seller sticker on this book unless it actually becomes a real one.[109]

---

[108] Is it any more ethical to try to sell mass quantities in the window to make the *New York Times* list? No, but if this book has hit that list by the time you read this, ta-da!

[109] By the way, if you know 10,000 friends who want this book, drop me a line.

41

Why Being a Work-at-Home Mom Is Bad for Business

BEING AUTHENTIC AND transparent with your business is a great idea. But what happens when we reveal too much about our business in our materials? Claiming to be a work-at-home business owner or—even more popular—a work-at-home mom can actually hurt more than it helps your business.

I've had people argue the point. They say that "this is what I am" and do not want to hide the fact that they are a parent or work from home, and that is just fine. I don't have an issue with your being a work-at-home person at all. The issue that I have is that it does not really come down to "what you are"; it is about how your potential market will perceive you.

There is an exception. If your market is other work-at-home parents, then saying you are one as well can be a great thing and it can work in all of your marketing materials. But outside of that market, claiming that you work from home, especially if you have children, can give people the perception that they may not be your priority as clients.

I am a work-at-home dad myself, so don't get me wrong. The majority of my clients are virtual, so I do my consulting work over the phone, online, or by going to a location to meet in person. I really have no need for expensive office space, fancy leather chairs, or a nameplate. But nowhere on my bio on my website will you see that I work from home. I leave it out purposefully, because it would then be open for interpretation by potential clients, who may have their own notions of what someone who works from home and has children can do. So when I see you leading with the fact that you're a work-at-home mom, I know for the most part that your children will be your priority.

If you mention you have three kids under six years old and you're home-schooling them, then I question when the work for me, the work I need done and am paying you to do, is going to get done. Some people will argue that being a mom automatically means that clients would think you're better at business, better at multitasking, at organizing, at delegation, and a whole bunch of other words. In reality, being a parent does not automatically make you anything except a parent. I want to hire you because of one thing—that you will get the job done.

I work from home, my assistant Karen works from home, and that all works great. I have designers and virtual assistants and writers who work for me virtually. I really don't care where they work, all I care about is that everything gets done. Being on social media and talking about having kids and everything that comes with it is great because it allows you to connect with other people who also have kids. I understand that. But on your formal business materials, on your website and brochures, the focus needs to be on your potential clients and what you can do for them.

42

Hello? Walmart?

EVERYONE HAS AN opinion about Walmart. It seems you either love them or hate them. Personally, I say it's up to you where you shop. I'm there all the time. It's easy, it's close, and I can get my cereal, a fanny pack, and cat food all in one stop—awesome. They're open late, prices are good, and everything I need is all under one roof. Remember, I am the world's laziest man.

Walmart can't be missed. The company has a strong brand that is supposed to be based on low prices and friendly service. Associates and greeters are encouraged to smile and say hello to every customer they see. This 10-foot rule was created by Walmart founder Sam Walton. On the Walmart website the company says that, "During his many store visits, Sam Walton encouraged associates to take this pledge with him: I promise that whenever I come within 10 feet of a customer, I will look him in the eye, greet him, and ask if I can help him."

Now that is my kind of corporate policy! I like feeling special, doesn't everybody? It is especially nice to see this kind of policy in such a huge store. Doesn't get any bigger than Walmart. Did you know they have a cheer? They do, and here are a few lines from it (www.WalmartStores.com).

> Whose Walmart is it? It's my Walmart!
> Who's number one? The customer! Always!

After spending a lot of time pushing my cart around the place on many occasions, I started wondering whether this policy was really being put into place. Was Walmart being authentic and walking their talk? So I went undercover again. This time with a hidden camera in my cart, I went for a little shopping trip. Lionel Richie's "Hello" plays in the background in the video—epic really. You can watch the video for yourself here: http://bit.ly/4JICy5.

In total, I passed 17 Walmart employees and not one said hello to me. I don't think Sam would have been impressed. Written policy and core values are great for your business. They set the tone and they remind you, your employees, and your customers what you stand for, who you are. But they are only as good as your actions. If you can't take those policies and turn them into a real experience for your market, then you might as well not have them.

When you don't provide the customer experience that your brand is supposed to represent, a few things can happen. Your company comes off as inauthentic, and your market begins to doubt whether you stand by any of your values or your policies. You begin to create an experience gap where your market begins to be less and less happy with your service, and competitors can move in. When I think about Walmart, I think low prices, not friendly service. How about you? That's what I thought. That is because they don't walk their talk.

Even if you are a one-person show, you can learn from this. Being who you say you are as a businessperson is important. You are always representing your brand. Eventually, someone will hold you accountable for the core values you claim to represent. Be authentic, and if you say you're going to say hello, say it.

43

Idea Creation

As MODERN BUSINESS owners we tend to become overwhelmed by all the methods of information delivery available to us and forget the biggest point of them all. No matter how many new ways exist today to deliver content, it's the content itself that matters most. Remember the saying "content is king." If you do not have great content, it does not matter at all how you deliver it.

So how do we create quality content? It's simple. You can start with just a basic idea and turn it into an entire series of content. Write down right now the biggest problem you solve for your customer, the pain that you heal from your marketplace. If you are a chiropractor, that means you relieve physical pain; if you are a financial planner, then you relieve the pain of money problems down the road for your clients; and if you're a TV repair person, well, then you solve the problem of my television that isn't working. Anyone in any type of business can create content around marketplace pain.

Let's take the example of the TV repair person. Simply by coming up with a top-five list for your marketplace, you can start down the road of separating your company from your competition. By providing useful content, you go from being a service provider with a ton of competition to an expert in the industry. I would only call a TV repair person when my TV is broken, but I can learn from an expert in the TV business at any time. It changes my opportunity to engage with you from only during those critical pain points to placing you in front of me all the time.

This is where you want to be in any business—in front of your market positioned as an expert. You could write a list of the top-five things to look out for when buying a new TV. On that list you could include the main concerns everybody has when making such a large purchase. For example, should I buy an extended warranty from the store? What's the difference between plasma and LCD? What size of TV should I get for the type of room I have? Please notice that we are talking about creating knowledge-based content around the pain points of your market.

Now that you have your idea, it's time to write something down. Here are the three simple steps for writing great content on any subject: Use the three Ps—Point, Prove it, Perform it.

1. *Point means just that you state your main point.* So if I were a financial planner writing an article about the top-five ways to save money for retirement, I might start by talking about putting away a percentage of each paycheck into a separate account. So that's the first "P." That's my point.

2. *Prove means that you give an example or scenario of the point.* So when you are writing about the financial world, you would show an example or case study of Mr. and Mrs. Jones, who put away $100 per paycheck every year for 20 years and ended up with lots of money.

3. *Now you need to tell your readers how they can learn from the proof and make it happen for themselves.* For the "perform it" section of your article, you would give an easy way for your readers to execute the same action. In the financial planner scenario

you could mention that any bank will set up an automated biweekly deduction from your bank account to put into a low-risk investment fund.

And there we have great content! What's your point, prove it to me as a reader, and then show me how to perform it.

Our chiropractor could specialize in athletes and come up with the best five stretches to do before a game so you won't get hurt. He then would mention a certain hamstring stretch, show a visual example of it to prove it, and then tell you how to perform it yourself. Using this simple method you can create one heck of a top-five or top-ten list that is not only informative but also practical for the reader. String a few of these together on your blog, and without even knowing it you have positioned yourself as a darn good expert—and you don't even have to call yourself one. ☺

If you need help in organizing your ideas, I would suggest using something like a mind map that will visually help you organize anything from a blog post to an entire 64,000-word book like I did for the one you are reading. I use a free program called *FreeMind* (http://FreeMind.SourceForge.net), which allows me to use an organizational chart to organize thoughts and ideas. The software is amazing, free, easy to use, and really helpful when putting together articles, blog posts, or even planning videos. If you don't want to use a computer program to organize your ideas, just pick up a pen and paper. Map out some ideas for the projects you are currently working on and for those in the future. You can set up a plan and create content for quite a long time. For example, the mind map I used for this book is at www.UnMarketing.com/blog/wpcontent/uploads/2009/12/mindmap.jpg.

44

Idea Delivery

ONCE YOU FIGURE out what your idea is going to be, you have to take three things into consideration when you choose a method of delivery: (1) What are you comfortable with or good at doing? (2) How does your market prefer to learn or acquire new information? and (3) What kind of point are you trying to get across?

One of the biggest mistakes I see people making in terms of delivering content is that they use a method that doesn't suit them or that they just are not very good at. When you are trying to choose your method, I would suggest trying a few out and getting feedback from people you trust. See how each one feels to you when you read, listen, or watch it. Also, remember that just because you use one method the first time, this doesn't mean you can't try something new in the future. You can always ask for feedback from your customers after they have received something and see what they say.

For delivering content you have three different methods online: audio, video, or written. If audio is your thing, you can do anything from a five-minute audio-tip or a podcast[110] all the way to an audio

---

[110] Wikipedia defines a *podcast* as "a series of digital media files (either audio or video) that are released episodically and downloaded through web syndication." http://en.wikipedia.org/wiki/Podcast.

series that's delivered on CD or through MP3s. You set up an audio session the same way as we did with the articles previously, using the three Ps. Start with your point, prove it with an example, and then tell your audience how they can perform it themselves. It is fairly simple to record audio, and it should be smooth sailing to create small audio chunks at a time. If you come up with a top-five list for your marketplace, you could record each of them separately and then release them one at a time on your blog. The audio can be streamed or downloaded by your listeners, plus at the end you can combine all the files together for a larger series.

The two biggest things to pay close attention to when recording audio are sound quality and how appealing your voice is. Good sound quality comes from choosing the right tools for recording—the microphone you're using and the computer it's going into. Spend a few extra dollars on a half-decent microphone and the value to your recording will be exponential. I use one of the Plantronics headsets, which plugs directly into the microphone jack on my laptop. I chose not to go with the USB headset because a direct input into a microphone jack gave me the best sound quality possible.

When it comes to your voice, the best way to know if you're doing it well is to record one of your short segments and play it back and listen to it or to have a few trusted people listen and give you honest, real feedback. I know that listening to yourself is excruciating for most people, because how we actually sound is totally different from how we hear ourselves in our heads, but this is so important. Being able to be critical about your own work and being able to accept honest feedback from others is incredibly valuable in business.

Now, although no one may be able to change his or her entire voice, there are many ways we can improve our audio content. When you practice, pay attention to your pace, volume, and enunciation. Listen to other speakers and how they sound. What do you like about your favorite speakers, and what don't you like? Confidence is also a huge factor. Confidence in your voice as you practice and improve makes a tremendous difference in the final product. When I worked with a company that booked speakers for a large conference in Toronto, we always looked out for the combination of someone who knew what he or she was talking about and who could also deliver it in a convincing way. There was no shortage of people out there who could do one out of the two, but somebody who can do both is always in demand.

Ask anyone nowadays and that person will tell you that video is currently the biggest method in presenting content, and it will continue getting bigger. Because the cost of cameras has come down so greatly over the past few years, and as they have also become smaller and more mobile, more and more people are using video. You would think by now that everyone would be, but that is not the case. So why aren't more people recording? Well, for one thing it can be intimidating to try. In video, there is nowhere to hide. People watching will be able to tell when you are nervous. There are tons of factors to consider, such as lighting and sound quality and controlling what is going on in the background.

I need to tell you that you do not have to make a video, and you certainly do not have to do it right away. If the video hurdle is too big and it keeps you from engaging with your market, there are other methods of delivery. As you become more confident in your writing and your audio, video will seem like less of a jump. You need to have a lot more confidence to do video well than with the other two methods combined. And to tell you the truth, I among many other people prefer to read blog posts so we can scan them to pick out the ideas we like best or find most useful. With video, your audience is forced to go at your pace. So don't sweat it if video is not something you want to do now or at all.

If you are up to giving video a try, it is an amazing tool to connect on a personal level with your marketplace. As your potential customer, if I am not able to see you in person, then the next best way to begin building trust with me, or for me to learn from you, is to be able to look right in your eye via video. Video is also a great way to show your potential customers how to do something since they can see it. So if you are demonstrating something, such as the chiropractor who shows stretches, then video is great.

When you work with video, one of the major benefits is that you can really cover all three methods of content delivery. You can record video and upload it while you actually strip the audio from the video and make it an MP3 file people can listen to. You could then also have the audio transcribed and available as a PDF or just as a blog post. Understand, though, that each style of delivery won't transfer perfectly over to the next. If you are showing something in your video, relying on physical cues or visual examples, then obviously something important will be missing when you translate that to only audio.

The spoken word is different from the written word. I learned this very quickly while writing this book. The section you are reading right now I created using audio. I am actually speaking these words into a microphone using a voice-to-text software program (I use Dragon NaturallySpeaking). The software is typing out the words for me. If I wanted to create an audio version of the book, I have all the files available to me, which is pretty cool, but the process isn't perfect. All of the text files created from audio have to be edited so that they read properly. I think that the art of using one method to create another is something that could be practiced and improved over time. If you are filming a video and you know you want the audio to be able to stand on its own, then you can practice speaking accordingly.

If you think writing is what you do best and where your comfort level is, focus on writing the best content possible. One note about editing here: You do not need to focus on being the best editor possible. My job when I write a blog post is to write something that is compelling and informative and to show my passion for the subject and try to evoke emotion from the reader. My job is not to retake grade 12 English—I barely spell-check. I have some great people who are happy to help me, and I return the favor for them. The focus should be on bringing passion to your writing.

Focus your attention on what your reader is going to get out of this post and leave the rest to somebody who is outside of that emotion. Sometimes reading your own posts over and over again for grammar and spelling will mean that you never actually put them out there.[111]

When choosing your method, you also need to take into account what message you're trying to get across. If you're trying to do some kind of product demonstration, especially if it's online for software or websites, then using the combination of audio and video together can be really helpful. Recording only audio can be easier and less nerve-racking than doing it on video. A nice way to combine the advantages of video and the ease of audio is by doing a screen capture program like Camtasia, where you record your voice but it is heard over the images you are showing on screen— like flash video with a voice-over.

Lastly, consider your potential customers. How will they best take your message? Why not ask them what they would like to see? Or try out a few different methods and see which gives you the best reaction and feedback from your customers.

---

[111] Sadly, most of the time I upload a blog post and then have someone look at it. It makes me look like a moron, but luckily that's part of my brand. ☺

45

Doing In-Person Seminars

A GREAT WAY to share your knowledge and position yourself as an expert is by doing local seminars. You have created some great content for your market, so you are ready to share it! It is said that people's number-one fear is public speaking, even greater than dying. I think that may be a little far-fetched, but I understand the issue.

Your audience members are not really there to see you. They attend a seminar to gain useful information. Once you get the realization that it's not about you, it can take a little bit of the pressure off and allow you to focus on sharing great content. Your main goal for seminars shouldn't be to pitch people your service or product, but it should be that the audience leaves the seminar with usable practical information. This is what will position you as an expert to them.

This doesn't mean you shouldn't be doing a pull and stay at the end of the seminar, and I don't even have an issue with your pitching something at the end as long as you've given valuable information throughout the session. However, too many sessions are majority pitch and little content.

If you have not built a big platform yet and aren't well known in the area, you need to leverage off somebody else's audience. This could be your local Chamber of Commerce, a business networking group, or any local association. These kinds of local groups are always on the lookout for quality speakers. You won't get paid a fee to do the sessions for the most part, but when you're starting out your payment is exposure to your marketplace.

Locally, this is a great way to build a following, but I caution you on doing many free seminars outside of your local area. When you start getting known virtually, people will start asking you to present seminars at their events. What the general audience does not know about most of these events—especially many of the Internet marketing ones—is that the speaker not only speaks for free but is on the hook for travel, accommodations, and meal expenses. If you've ever gone to one of these events as an attendee and wondered why some of the speakers pitch so hard during their seminar, it's because they are already in the hole the second they step on the stage. Three or four nights' hotel accommodation and a return flight, among other things, can mean that the speakers you're looking at are already down $1,000, if not more, before they even open their mouths.

As the audience, remember that the conference organizer may be putting a lot of pressure on the speaker. Often, the organizer will get half the revenue from anything sold at the event. If the speaker does not sell, then he or she will not be asked back to future events. So not only would the speaker have to sell $1,000 worth of product from the stage to break even, but he or she would actually have to sell $2,000 worth of product from the stage to break even.

As a speaker, if you are looking at an event that you were going to anyway and were willing to pay to attend, then being offered a speaking slot is a great way to attend the conference for free, plus you get exposure in front of your potential market. That is a winning situation that can help out your business on your own terms. However, speaking at many seminars for no pay outside of your local market is a quick way to go broke. Not to mention that the organizer will usually book 15 to 20 speakers over three days to maximize the event's potential revenue, so the audience is getting pitched 15 to 20 times in those three days. When audience participants are over-pitched, they become less and less interested in what you have to say and less likely to become future customers of yours.

The requirement to sell from the stage means that many conference organizers don't necessarily pick the best content providers for seminars. They choose the best closers, the ones they've heard who can generate the most money from stage. And when you do not deliver sales from the stage, you will not be asked back.

This setup does not benefit the attendees. It hurts the longevity of the conference from year to year and turns off many people from seminars that are actually really good. These conferences are usually sold as low-ticket items from $97 to $497, which is usually your first indication that the event will be pitch-heavy. In-person seminars cost a lot of money to implement. The organizers need to secure a half-decent hotel and rent rooms, organize food, and so forth. Organizing seminars is their business, and they are in it to make money, not necessarily for the betterment of the industry.

Recently there has been a surge of great events such as Pod-Camp and BarCamp that are low cost but high value. If you want to find out which events are the best to go to as an attendee or a speaker, simply ask around on Twitter or Facebook, where people are honest with their opinions.

What happens with many of the bad events is that the organizer books 20 or so speakers and allows them to be affiliates for the conference, meaning that they will be earning a percentage of the revenue for every ticket they sell to the event.[112] The problem then is that when you get known as a speaker and begin to speak

---

[112] Really? You're going to share in the revenue I create for you? You're too kind.

more frequently, in some of the speaker agreements with these events your contract will include that you will promote it. You will have to agree to promote their event X amount of times to your list. Event organizers are even beginning to mandate how many tweets you have to send out about it before the event. When you promote too many events, you end up exhausting your list. Your list will not want to hear about too many events, and then when the events end up being heavy on pitch and light on content, you will lose your list. Think of how hard you worked to gain your following. Do you really want to lose them with forced promotions for events when you disagree with how they are organized?

One of the other reasons that organizers book such a high number of speakers is because they figure each of the 20 or so speakers can bring in 10 paid attendees, which will bring 200 people into the audience. I feel that it is the organizer's job to bring people into the event. As a speaker, I bring my content to the event, the value of giving paying attendees something to see, hear, and learn. I do not pitch from stage. Valuable content should be your greatest sales tool when you work to position yourself in front of your market as an authority. You should be encouraged to give as much value in the hour as you have to give—not to hold back so you can sell more at the end.

I remember getting an e-mail from a conference organizer last year for an event where I was scheduled to speak. The e-mail said that as speakers we collectively needed to pull together and start promoting the heck out of the event because registrations were so low. I wrote them back to inform them that I was always happy to mention when I would be speaking at the event in their area; however, I am not a salesperson for their event. After going back and forth with a few heated e-mails, I ended up removing myself from the event. It was clear that the content that speakers were bringing to the event was not valued and, therefore, it was not the kind of thing with which I wanted my company associated.

I do understand the idea of bartering your speaking skills for exposure. It is okay with me, as long as you feel you're getting equal value back for what you're doing. Please, just make sure that you don't go into so much debt for the event that you feel pressured to sell from the stage. If you have to make a certain number of sales just to break even, it is going to show in your presentation. Your speaking will come off as inauthentic and pushy and ruin whatever great content you shared during the seminar.

46

Tele-Seminars

ONCE YOU HAVE started to build a platform and a following, a great way to further position yourself as an expert is by doing tele-seminars. One nice thing about doing a tele-seminar as opposed to an in-person event is that nobody knows how many people have shown up. Having five people attend an in-person event that has 50 chairs set up is embarrassing. Having five people show up to a tele-seminar, although not ideal, will go unnoticed. So these seminars are a great place to practice and gain confidence in your speaking and in your content.

You want to ensure that with tele-seminars you give stand-alone value to it. Way too many of these events are pitch-focused, where you don't really even give content, or maybe just a hint of content, and then spend the remainder of the time trying to convince the listener to buy something.

I remember calling in to listen to my first tele-seminar eight years ago. It was run by one of the big-name motivational speakers. So I blocked off the time on my calendar, took away time from my family (it was in the evening), and dialed into the conference phone number. The first 10 minutes consisted of the speaker getting the phone-call attendees all revved up for the call itself, and pretty much the remainder of the hour was about how you can succeed in life by taking advantage of this great opportunity. The great opportunity that was being offered on this call was to sign up for their high-priced coaching program.

I got off that call feeling angry and sort of frustrated that I had trusted this person with my time. If you take nothing else from this book, take the importance of valuing other people's time, which is another reason for never cold-calling, putting on pitch-heavy events, and generally not respecting people for the time committed to you. I vowed that day never to run a tele-seminar like that myself. I promised myself that if somebody chose to honor me with their gift of time that when that person got off the phone he or she would get easy-and-quick tips to implement the knowledge that I was offering.

When you set up your own tele-seminar, decide whether you want to do a free or paid version. They both have benefits. A free tele-seminar will get a much higher response, but also know that your attendance rate of those who signed up compared to those who actually phone in will be fairly low. On the other hand, doing a paid tele-seminar will give you an audience of people who are a little more qualified to potentially take the next step with you for your products or services. You also have to look at perceived value. Some people may not sign up for a free tele-seminar assuming it'll be pitch-heavy, because free seminars usually are. And be careful with paid tele-seminars: Even if someone has paid a small fee like $15, attendees are expecting value from that. Creating a pitch-heavy tele-seminar where people have to pay to listen is a sure way to get many refund requests. Paid tele-seminars work best when they are about a focused topic. Free ones work well when the topic is more general and it is in the upsell of the seminar where the customer will have access to more depth. Most people do not have an issue with pitching something at the end of a free tele-seminar or even a paid one as long as the value has been given prior to the pitch. It's a great way for people to get a taste of how you are on the phone. People can hear your voice, bringing you one step closer to establishing a better trust relationship with them in the long run.

Coming up with topics can be as simple as asking people on your mailing list. Come up with five great topically based titles per tele-seminar and ask your list members to vote on which one they're most interested in. Use an online survey service where you can see the results immediately. By getting people to rank their interests in each of the five titles, you get some valuable information. Not only does this show you where your market's interests lie, but in turn people will also feel like they have contributed to the topic you choose. This makes them feel valued and involved and gives them a little more to buy in.

For example, if you are an accountant and your list consists of small business owners, come up with five different titles that address some of their biggest fears or desires. Titles like "Five Things You Can Do To Reduce Your Tax Obligation" can go over well when tax season is approaching. Even better, make the topic evergreen (meaning, always fresh and interesting) by switching it to "Five Things You Can Do To Increase Your Bottom Line in the Next 30 Days." You don't even need to have the entire session laid out when asking your list. The key is that once list members choose their favorite, you have to ensure that whatever you are revealing on that tele-seminar is great content. I did my first tele-seminar about the six keys to viral marketing about six years ago, where I revealed a lot of the information that you can find in the viral marketing section of this book. I gave a lot of solid content to my customers and, at the end, after telling everybody how to make their own viral movies, I made them the offer that my company could make it for them. That one tele-seminar was the nucleus for sales for the next five years.

When I did my first tele-seminar, I really didn't have a list at that time. I created a topic that I thought was interesting, wrote some bullet points of what people would get out of it, and then mentioned it to a few of my colleagues who I thought would benefit from the content. I offered a referral fee to whoever mentioned the seminar on their list. Even though the tele-seminar was free, any sale that came out of it would be credited to that person and he or she would get a cut.

When trying to approach list owners to do a tele-seminar, it really helps to have a relationship with them first. I get people asking me all the time to promote their seminars to my list. For motivational-theme seminars, I have hundreds of thousands of subscribers. But most of the time I don't even know that person. I, or any other list owner of significant size, has given a lot of time and resources to building a list. We didn't build it so you can benefit from it. There is also a lot of trust involved—my list trusts me, and I am not about to lose that trust by recommending something less than great.

For people with whom I have a relationship, who I trust and know they will provide quality information, it is an easy decision for me. Just as it was an easy decision for this person to have me do a tele-seminar for her list. So if you're going to approach other list owners, have a topic ready with some bullet points and let them know what you're willing to offer them for it.

47

Tele-Summits

ONE OF THE newest trends out there is not the tele-seminar but the tele-summit. This is where someone puts together a series of tele-seminars usually under one common topic.

Generally, the organizer will contact 10 to 20 experts in a certain field to speak on a common topic. The tele-summit is marketed to potential customers in a really smart way. Many of these events allow you to sign up for the event for free, under the condition that you have to phone in and listen to the live calls. Of course, over the course of a three- or four-day tele-summit, most people will not have time to listen to 20 or so one-hour phone calls. At this point, they are usually offered an upgrade. Either on the sales page, or after they sign up for the free access, a gold or platinum or another fancy metal name will show up to offer an upgrade to various packages.

These upgrades vary. One option would be access to the MP3 recordings of all the sessions. Another upgrade can be PDF transcripts of all the sessions. The top-level upgrade would be getting all MP3 recordings, PDF transcripts, and everything on CD and a printed binder. I actually really like this method. It allows you to give content away for free but also allows you to make some revenue for people who want to digest the information on their own time. If you end up wanting to run your own tele-summit, which is something you can put together once you build relationships with other experts in your industry, this would be the best way you could sell it.

Bringing in dynamic speakers is the most important part of creating a great tele-summit. When you are organizing one, you need to think of the value points you offer to speakers. In a tele-summit, one of the selling points to speakers is that they can do the talk from anywhere that they like; they don't even have to leave home. It's a pretty good deal—calling in for an hour they do their talk and become aligned with other experts in the field in this great project. This is also true for many of the conferences out there where speakers are asked to contribute for free in exchange for exposure and the ability to potentially pitch something at the end of their talk. Some will also include the always wonderful incentive of earning a commission for every person the speaker refers to the event.

Even though the medium has changed from in-person to virtual, most of these seminars fall into the same problems as live ones. Lack of great content, too much pitching, and content where the person sounds like a robot reading a script all happen in tele-summits and seminars as often as they do at live events. The difference with online events is that here, unlike in live events where there are costs to rent venues and travel, the organizer now incurs almost no risk when running the event. Short of having to put up a web page ad and the time to organize speakers for the event, there is little to no risk to the advertiser.

This is further complicated by the low barrier to entry for running one of these things—really anyone can do it. Many of the organizers are using the mentality of the in-person event, bringing in many speakers, taking a percentage of sales, and making speakers promote it.

To demonstrate these expectations by organizers and how speakers can be treated, I would like to share with you an experience I had. I recently got an e-mail from the organizer of a tele-summit that I had agreed to be a part of. The e-mail felt underhanded. Here is a part of it:

> A few of the speakers have contacted us asking us to give them an update on the number of participants to the conference. We have hesitated to provide a response as unfortunately we are unhappy with the number of registrations.
>
> One of the reasons we invited you to contribute to the conference is because we know that you walk your talk and we hold you up as an example of an expert who knows how to build their business. What we noticed is that all of the registrations were coming from the choice community and a disproportionate few have come from your supportive efforts.

As you can probably tell, I blew a gasket about this one. They are pretty much saying, "Hey, we've been doing all the work here, you need to pull up your socks and start promoting. You are asked to speak at this event because you have a lot of followers on Twitter and a big mailing list; we expect you to make sales."

My reply to the organizers stated my disappointment with the e-mail, and the sentiment kindly expressed my feelings toward speaking at their event. In their further reply they mentioned I may have misinterpreted what they had written, so apparently it was my fault again. This was the last tele-summit I ever agreed to be on. I used to think it was a compliment to be asked to be on somebody's seminar, but sadly I realized that these events are a dime a dozen, and most organizers are hunting for the sales that I can generate. I will still do them from time to time but only for people I know, trust, and like. You see how that comes back again? Know. Trust. Like.

48

How and Why I Created a Summit Ebook Instead

ONE OF THE advantages of all of the networking that I have done over the past year or so, especially on Twitter, is that I have gotten to know and build friendships with many amazing speakers, authors, and coaches. Because I am all three, these are the people I often gravitate toward. I wanted to do something collectively with a group of people who were also experts in these fields. My goal was to create a high-value item that would share the knowledge of some great people who were friends of mine. The product would expose these experts and the knowledge and experience they had to share with others, and the best part was, I would be giving it away for free.

I could have gone the tele-summit route because it was gaining so much momentum at the time, but I really didn't want to do that for a few reasons. In a tele-summit you are limited to a certain number of time slots during the summit. I didn't want a schedule to mean that a great person I loved would not be able to share their knowledge with people.

One of the ways that tele-summit organizers get around having their speakers dictated by a schedule is by prerecording seminars and then playing it as "live." Often the organizers will not disclose this, and I feel the omission is a little inauthentic, so I was not going to do this with my project.

It was also really important to me that the product I was creating did not have to rely on the contributors to promote it to be successful. To successfully do a tele-summit with a limited amount of time, you need as many people as possible working to promote it. I was not about to make promoting the project to their list a condition for them to take part. I truly wanted the contributors to share their content and then not feel obligated to do anything more. I wanted them for their minds, not their lists.

I had to think of an idea that would not be a time burden for the contributors, that would work for the speakers, authors, and coaches' market I wanted to place myself in front of, and that would create so much value that it would almost be a no-brainer for people to pass along to other people.

This is why I decided to use an ebook format called *If you could go back*. The premise was simple. For each area that a contributor was an expert in, I would ask them a simple and important question: If you could go back to the start of your career, what three things would you do differently? It's actually a really great question to ask yourself to reflect on what you've learned. The answers are useful to pass on to other people who are new or even currently in the field.

I gave the option to people I wanted to include in the book to either e-mail their answers or give them to me over the phone. Personally, when I am asked to contribute to projects like these myself, which happens all the time, I don't usually send it back if it has to be an e-mail. I just get tired of typing. Don't make me jump through hoops to give you content. Nor did I want to be transcribing and typing as if I were doing a phone interview—I want to enjoy their answers.

Because most of these people were friends of mine by this point, we really had a good time. The majority of the contributors chose the option of a phone call. I ended up using Skype to do the phone calls, and more than half the people who contributed also used Skype. According to Wikipedia, Skype is

> a software application that allows users to make voice calls over the Internet. Calls to other users of the service and, in some countries, to free-of-charge numbers, are free, while calls to other landlines and mobile phones can be made for a fee. Additional features include instant messaging, file transfer, and video conferencing.

The phone quality is excellent, as good if not better than any phone I have ever used for interviewing. When both parties are using Skype, there is a special program called *Pamela*, which is a third-party software program that you run alongside Skype that will record the call. I then took the MP3 file recording that was generated from the conversation and had it transcribed.

When I initially launched the ebook I simply put together these transcribed conversations. What I learned quickly was that the spoken word did not always translate well into the written word without editing. I feel that the lack of editing at the beginning may have kept some people who were willing to promote the project from passing it along. I did complete this step later, when one of the people who downloaded the ebook read it. Traci Feit Love[113] dropped me a line to say how great the content was but that she felt it was not of consistent quality. She offered to edit it for me at no charge, in exchange for a recommendation if I liked her work. I thought this was genius of her! She did a fantastic job and I ended up recommending her to all the people who contributed to the ebook. She got business right away from one of them,

---

[113] www.TraciFeitLove.com

and I ended up hiring her to edit another book I wrote that was more than 20,000 words.

After getting the recordings transcribed, I had my assistant contact each contributor for a photo and a bio to add to each page. The results were amazing! I had collected more than 40 contributors and 120 pages of great reflective content. You can go check it out for yourself at BuildYourFollowing.com.

Some of the contributors did end up promoting the ebook because they believed in the quality of the project and the value to potential readers. I also made an affiliate link for it available to them, not because there was some kind of upsell when they downloaded it, but if the reader ended up buying something from me down the road, the contributor would then get credit for it.

If you go to BuildYourFollowing.com, you will also notice a few important things. I decided people would have to double opt-in to receive the ebook, which was sort of their payment to get it. I could have just given the ebook away for free with no opt-in, but that would mean that I lost my pull-and-stay possibilities with them. People who opted in were also added to my newsletter list, of which they were informed in a video on the website.

You never want to add anyone to any kind of list that person didn't ask for or know he or she was going to get. If you want to have a look for yourself, go to the website and sign up for the ebook. Have a look at the process I use to ensure that people confirm their e-mail addresses. Building a list was only one goal for this project. I really wanted people to read the ebook because of the content. I didn't want them to sign up and then forget it was there.

After the first video, when someone clicks on to sign up for the ebook, up pops a second video thanking that person for requesting the ebook and asking that he or she please go check e-mail or the spam folder to ensure the customer bought it. I want to make sure that people get the ebook. Confirmation rates are so hideously low nowadays that you need to do everything possible to make sure people immediately confirm.

Once they confirm,[114] there is a third video along with the downloadable link that thanks them again and also encourages them to pass along the ebook. They are encouraged to pass along the website rather than sending people a PDF copy of the ebook so that their contacts will also receive ebook updates. I'm constantly updating the ebook with new people contributing; therefore, I can continue to send out the fresh content to everyone who subscribes. This is currently getting me a 90 percent confirmation rate, which is about 40 percent higher than most lists.

If this is something you want to do within your industry, you can use this exact technique. Go ahead and use it for real estate agents or financial planners or professional organizers, or whatever it is you want to be an authority in. You know other people in your industry who would be willing to contribute. If you would rather not have your direct competitors in the ebook, then find people outside of a geographic area who can contribute to it. For example, if you are a real estate agent, you may not want other real estate agents from your area in your ebook. You might consider getting other agents from across the country to mention three things that home sellers do to get the most money for their home. You could interview people in general, asking them what would they do differently if they went back and bought their first house.

You just have to make sure that you promote and sell the ebook properly, both to the contributors and to the potential readers. I suggest that you make it as simple and easy as possible for your contributors to share, but give them the choice of how they can give you content. Demonstrate your appreciation to them by giving them a bio and exposure to people in lists they would never be in front of. After all, without their content, your project would not

---

[114] Feel free to opt out once you see this process; it'll only make me cry a little bit.

be valuable. Make sure that it is filled with great content. Sell it to the market as a content-rich ebook and it is sure to do really well.

This is why I didn't go after the most well-known speakers or coaches or authors—mainly because many of them would just have a pitch-heavy contribution. I wanted pure, honest content.

49

Viral Marketing

VIRAL MARKETING HAS many names. You can have a code name for it called *Buzz*. It can be WOM, which stands for word of mouth. It can be called *pass-along rates*. It goes out there and it gets watched. It goes out there and it just goes and grows. It's the art of having other people tell their friends about you.

You can call it whatever you want. Going viral is what we all want, right? How about if I told you a way to get hundreds, thousands, or millions of people to talk about you? I have a little bit of an ego myself. I dig that. I like people doing that, talking about me and what I do. That's what we want; that's the whole goal. How do we get people to feed the system, to be a part of our community?

People use the term *viral marketing* a lot. They say things like, "Oh, I had a virus last month on my computer. I don't want to learn this, Scott. It was wicked. It said it was the anti-virus '09 and it screwed everything up." Viral marketing has nothing to do with viruses. Viral simply means when a host person gets it out there and it spreads. Now one of the dangers with this kind of marketing is that once it goes, you can't stop it, and we'll talk all about that and what's horrible about not being able to stop it.

Viral marketing is pretty basic. It does not matter what kind of method you use, whether it is YouTube or "micro viral" like we find on Twitter. It doesn't matter what the medium is.

There are four secrets to successful viral marketing that we talk about in this section of the book. Secret number one is to pick one of the following areas to focus on: the message either is funny, it has the WOW factor, or it evokes emotion.

1. *The message is funny.* I don't mean funny like the dude at the party who thinks he's funny and you don't want to talk to the guy. That's awkward. He's usually drinking some kind of spritzer in the corner. Nobody talks to him, and he says, "You know, I've got a great knock-knock joke for you."[115] So it's got to be funny. I mean hold-your-gut laughing. Funny is really the most difficult of the three to pull off; you just can't fake being funny. It's really tough to do, and if you try too hard, it's actually rather difficult for most people to look at.

2. *The message has that WOW factor.* I don't mean wow as in, "Wow, you got new shoes. That's cool." I mean, "Holy sweet mother, did you see what just happened?!" Usually that's how YouTube videos go around a lot. It's the reporter talking about car crashes at the same time that a car crashes behind him. You know it's viral when in your mind you say, "I've got to show this to somebody." That's viral. That's what we're talking about here. Making something so amazing that viewers feel they have to tell everybody they talk to about it. It is not easy to do, but if you can harness it, nothing is more powerful. Wow can also be something that has incredible value. This is one of the reasons that writing content-rich blog posts is a good idea to get word of mouth going for your blog.

---

[115] No joke is ever good when it starts with knock-knock by the way.

3. *The message evokes emotion.* Does the message make you feel something? Do you care about it? This is really the one that I think you can harness. This is the one that I've mostly harnessed myself. Emotional means that it makes your hair stand up on your neck. It makes you think. Anything like that—motivational, inspirational, those types of things. When it evokes emotion, you then automatically qualify in your minds, "Who else do I want to show this to?"

The emotion can actually be yours, where you reveal something personal within a blog post, video, and so forth. I did one of those "25 Things You Didn't Know About Me" posts, and it was one of the most-read and reacted-to things that I have ever written.[116]

Without one of these three themes in play, you lose any motivation for people to send things around, outside of outright bribery. A fourth way to get people to send things out is to give them incentives (e.g,. commissions, as an affiliate, prize giveaways for the most tweets), but it's not natural and they usually have a short life span.

Secret number two is critical, so listen closely: Viral marketing is *not* about you. I cannot stress this enough. Your viral project, your viral attempt, is not about you. It's about your audience. When I say be funny, I don't mean you think it's funny. I mean your audience thinks it's funny. When I tell you about emotion, I mean what will make your audience feel, think, and react.

You do not even get to call it viral. I have seen people on Twitter talking about their new viral project. You are not the one who says it goes viral. It is not your call. I get e-mails all the time from people asking me to go and check out their new viral video! Then I go and follow the link to have a look and their "viral movie" has

---

[116] www.Un-Marketing.com/blog/2009/12/06/25-things-you-didnt-know-about-me/

nine views! That's the "viral" you're talking about? Am I right? Oh, and you're training people on how to produce viral videos? That's great, awesome, wow. I just threw up on my laptop. It's ridiculous. You do not get to say what goes viral, I do! I'm kidding, I don't.[117] Your market and your audience dictate it. It is not about you. Meaning, please don't put a picture of you in it.

The day you start talking to your audience and it's about them, that's the day that business really happens. Everything, I don't care if it's video or articles (which can go viral, too), or if it's a blog post, make it about your marketplace, not about you.

As an example of viral marketing I would like to share with you the first video that I did that went viral. This was way back in the day—about five or six years ago. This is the first-ever viral video that I made, and I didn't really know what I was in for. The *Time Movie* is really a glorified slide show (TheTimeMovie.com) that is meant to have the viewer feel that life is too short to take for granted and all we have is time, so it's up to us to spend it wisely. It is a nice message, yet was a stand-alone one that really had nothing to do with my products. This allowed the viewer to believe it was all about them.

The *Time Movie* is a perfect example of a video that went viral because of the emotion it evoked in its audience. I launched it in 2004. I think it was October of 2004 to be exact. I said to myself, "I am going to do this. I'm going to get it out there. I'm going to harness the power of the Internet!" I got a website designed and I put it up, and then nothing happened. I really thought I would just get sales because I put the website up. Apparently nobody got the memo that I put the website up there, and so I got nothing.

The *Time Movie* has now been viewed more than 4 million times. People are watching it right now. How cool is that? You are here reading and they are there and they're watching it. So it's

---

[117] Only sometimes.

perpetual! Viral marketing, when done right, is the most perpetual marketing machine you can have—perpetual meaning that no effort has to be put into it any longer. That's what I like. That's what I want to do. I want to do something once and have it go a million times. That's the whole point. I got more than a quarter million newsletter subscribers. I screwed them all up, which I will tell you all about shortly.[118]

I started out in motivational speaking. ScottStratten.com is my motivational speaking site. When I launched the *Time Movie*, I did it to get more speaking jobs and in turn got more than 1,000 speaker kit requests. If you're a speaker yourself, you understand the significance of that. Because when I was starting out, I would have been happy with four, five, or even one kit request. I would have been happy if one person had said,

"We want you to speak."

"Okay, yes I will! How much are you going to pay me?"

"We don't pay."

"Okay, do I get free lunch?"

"No."

"That's okay, I'll bring my lunch."

"And you have to pay to get in."

"Okay."

You know what we most want in life, right? We just want validation. That's human nature. I just wanted to be validated. Somebody wanted to hear what I had to say! And apparently that meant it was at the library at 3:00 in the afternoon with seven people there—and five of those were relatives, and two worked at the

---

[118] Yay! Other people's pain!

library and were on their lunch. Anyway, I made more than $100,000 in product revenue from the movie. I also screwed that up royally, but that's coming up.

Today, there are 1,540 inbound links from Yahoo! and more than 400 from Google. If you put TheTimeMovie.com into the search you'll see that. Again, I didn't plant any of those. The audience decided. And this was four or five years ago! I can't even imagine what would happen if I launched it fresh today with blogs the way they are and Twitter and Facebook. None of that was happening to the extent that it is today. I don't even want to know what would have happened, because I'll start crying.

FastCompany talked about it. The *Wall Street Journal* talked about it. Again, nothing to do with me. That was just me sitting there playing my Xbox at home and FastCompany calls:

"Hi, yeah, I can talk to you. Oh, you think I'm important? Okay, hi!"

The company validated me and I got in there because of the popularity of the movie—because it went viral. Now I can put in my bio "as featured in the *Wall Street Journal* and FastCompany." It doesn't change who I am. Validation of me and my work by media such as these two gives clout. In this case, instant clout. Clout is almost instant positioning as an expert on the hierarchy of buying.

You want to build a business and have people flock to you? Position yourself. Position yourself as the bringer of emotion that your market wants to feel. I don't care what the emotion is, as long as it is about your market. The emotion can be success, financial windfall, doing daily business, meeting a significant other, or being a better parent. If you are the provider of that emotion for these people, you will have business for the rest of your life. No matter what state the economy is in, emotion always sells. We overcomplicate viral marketing to the nth degree. It doesn't have to be hard.

The Landing Page

Here is the key. The *Time Movie* has had 4 million views,[119] but views don't mean anything unless you can keep these people in front of you and continue to engage with them. After someone watches the movie, something else needs to happen to bring them in—the landing page.

For the *Time Movie*, the landing page says this:

Sometimes, just sometimes we all need that reminder. The reminder that life is too short to waste and too precious to leave to routine. We need a reminder to give more time for families and friends and just as importantly, ourselves. 'Work your life' is that reminder. It's a gentle nudge to get you remembering what's important to you. It's free and it's the kind of thinking you'll find adding joy to your life. To start receiving these precious reminders just twice a month, enter your e-mail address below and click on the button that says 'I deserve more.'

The landing page continues the emotive theme of the movie, it connects to the feelings the audience is having right then, and it doesn't ask for too much. If you liked the movie and you saw that landing page come up, would you want to take the next step? Of course, that is just the point. The landing page is where you take the emotion to the next step. The movie is not about you. The landing page is where you begin to introduce yourself. You bridge the emotion your audience is having into his or her taking one step.

Please look back at the wording and see that I am not selling anything on the landing page. That is probably the worst thing you can do. "I hope you enjoyed the movie, now give me money." Not pitching too soon is part of helping the project go viral. If the

---

[119] Four million views and $5 will get me a Starbucks coffee.

landing page hits at the end, this screws up the emotion, and the audience won't pass it along. It would be like seeing a performance and at the end the singer misses a note. What do you remember? The bad note.[120]

There was a time when my website was all about me. I changed it to be all about you, about my market, and potential and current customers. Originally, the landing page had 11 choices along with my name and my picture. It drastically took viewers from a movie about them to a page about me. A great guy online, Paul Myers,[121] helped me rewrite the site and make it about the viewer. As an example of how important harnessing emotion is, remember the button. A change from "submit" to "I deserve more!" on the button increased conversions by 8 percent. You can almost hear the viewers at their computer clicking the button and thinking, "Damn right, I deserve more!" Continue the experience all the way down to the button. The landing page converted at 24 percent. That means that 24 percent of viewers converted into my newsletter. Of course, I don't have even remotely that many now, because I messed it up, but you're going to have to wait just a little bit longer for that.

When you are designing your landing page, remember to keep it simple. On the *Time Movie* landing page, the disclaimer at the bottom says, "Your address will never be rented or sold, period." It's that simple. That is my legal statement.[122] That's all I do. You can say something like, "I hate spam as much as you; I'd never do that to you." Whatever you like is great, but just give your audience that reassurance.[123]

---

[120] I won't—trust me—I won't sing for you. To those who have seen my Twitter video, you don't want me to sing either.

[121] www.TalkBizNews.com

[122] Now, I'm sure it's not following laws of exactly the way I have to do it. I just don't care.

[123] And then sell their e-mail address if you want. I'm just kidding, don't sell anybody's e-mail. Unless it's a good price, then, hey, you know. We'll talk.

Secret number three to being successful in viral marketing is to properly define your success. What do you want this viral marketing thing to do? This is where people often miss the mark and lose out. People say that they just want their project to go viral, but they don't think about the why. Viral marketing is the best thing you can do to position yourself, your business, or your product in front of your market, but you've got to say what you want.

Do you want to build a following? Building your list is the most powerful thing that viral can do. Do you want sales? Viral marketing can work for sales, and it has many times. I have had clients who have created sales from it, but I don't suggest that sales be your goal, because you can turn off many people trying it. Do you want to build relationships? You can go viral and build relationships with other people in your industry. Twitter is a great example of that.

A note about building your list. Did any of you send out a newsletter in the late 1990s? Do you remember what it was like when people actually opened your newsletter? And got it, and read it, and there were no spam filters or traps and you didn't have to spell words like sells with $ and a weird character so it just gets through the filter? That's back in the day. Today I want to create a newsletter that gets opened, end of story. I want people to recognize my name and say, "Scott's written me something and I'm opening it." That's what you want. You don't want a huge list. You want an engaged list. The gold isn't in the list anymore. The gold is in the engagement of your lists and the relationship you have with the list members.

The content of your newsletter is so important. If you are just feeding your list pitches and pitches and more affiliate pitches every month, you are going to lose people, fast. You can't come back to your readers in every issue and say, "This is the greatest program!" with your affiliate link attached and then say the same in the next issue for a different product with another affiliate link.

I subscribe to about four newsletters now. I used to subscribe to 400. You all lost me. And when you lose me once, I'm not coming back. What are your followers worth to you? Don't try to sell them right at the start. Build the engagement with them.

Secret number four to success in viral marketing is choosing the right method to create and distribute your project. Depending on your goals for your viral marketing project, you now need to decide what process you are going to use to get there. Your success is defined by what method you're going to use. When making this decision, there are many things to consider; here are a few options for you. Just a note here: No one process is going to be the be-all or end-all for your business. Not one single technique is going to take your business from "here to here," end of story, with one tip. Please take that into account.

So here are a few options that I have found successful for me: flash video, live video, streaming video, and social media. Let's talk about each one a little more.

Flash Video

Flash video, like I used in the *Time Movie*, can be a great tool for building a list and potentially making sales. It can be a great start to relationship building and engagement. Flash is great for presenting an emotion. You have three choices if you want to go this route. The first is to learn how to create something within flash, which is hard to do and should be left to professional designers, although programs like iMovie for Mac allow you to use flash technology without having to learn it. Second, you could hire somebody to do it. Even though my company makes these now, I started by going to companies like Elance.com to outsource their creation. Third, a new option is to use a website like Animoto. com that will create these types of slideshows with effects and music. You plug in the text and pictures/video clips, and the site renders it with fancy animation and style. The results can be remarkable.

Over the past few years, we have made 65 flash videos. If you have seen one of those types of videos, 95 percent of the time we made it. We have found that it is best to use as many words as needed to get your point across, but no more. In my experience, the ideal has been about 10 to 12 scenes to be most effective. A length of three to four minutes is best.

File size is also important to keep an eye on. We have found that one to two megs in size is best. People will not wait more than, I'd say, an eighth of a second for something to load nowadays. It's the ADD nation. We're all like gnats with no attention span. Nowadays, people will not wait for your viral message. It's not about you, it's them!

To begin, you create a storyboard. It's like writing an essay outline: Scene 1 – opening. End Scene – ending. Then you fill up the middle and you are all set!

Live Video

Live video is just that: you on camera. If live video works for you, then it is really good for building a list. You can build one-to-one relationships using it, and you can create sales from it. So you can cover all three of your possible goals for viral marketing. Just remember that live video is much harder to pull off than a flash video because it's going to be you on camera.

Live video really hooks your audience and can help connect you one-to-one with people—on a relationship level. If you are your brand, you need to be doing live video. End of story. I have never found a method more effective or more scalable than live video. If you want to position yourself in front of your audience, do a good live video. I don't mean live as in "streaming" where it buffers and you're getting a headset on and trying to make it work properly and it doesn't. I mean you are going to record something so that it is a person versus flash, a person versus animation. It does not have to be hard or cost much money. It really doesn't. You don't have to spend much money to make live video successful for you and your business.

Delivery is the key. You cannot just post your video on You-Tube and buy your limo because you are going to be so huge in the industry! YouTube is absolutely horrible for your business. Yeah, you heard that right.[124] Depending on your goals for your viral project, YouTube is the worst possible tool for your business. If you are looking just to accumulate as many views as possible, and that's your ego trip of the day, then YouTube is for you. Every day you can check in and say, "Yay! Look! Twelve more views! Awesome!" I do that sometimes. Only sometimes, when I'm feeling really low.

If you like the interaction of comments, fine, but remember, when you open up your video to the world, the world comes. This includes people who insult your video and don't like it. Then you may get defensive and comment back, "How dare you? This is my video page, not yours!" Actually, it is YouTube's video page. They own it and therefore anybody can comment on it. So, relax. You need a thick skin if you're going to be out there. And that goes for anything to do with social media today, by the way. Twitter, Face-book, blogs, anything. As mentioned earlier in the Trolls section, many of those people aren't worth your time. So define your suc-cess. If you just want views, then go nuts. YouTube it up!

One of my own viral videos was ImBreakingUpwithTheLeafs .com, where I got so frustrated with my lifelong hockey team, the Toronto Maple Leafs, that I finally decided to end this madness and mockingly sit down to dinner with them and end it once and for all. It cost me nothing to make. I was sitting on my couch and

---

[124] I'm going to get sued by YouTube. Please don't tweet that. They're going to read it and sue me. Oh, tweet it anyway.

thought, "I'm going to make a video." I grabbed my little camera, my little Sony camera, not like an HD thing. I went into the kitchen, got the tripod, sat down, and started. That was it.[125] I didn't hold a staff meeting to talk about it. I just did it! It took me less than one hour, from idea to filming to uploading to registering the URL. That's it.

I e-mailed it out to two bloggers who didn't know me. One blogger was an Ottawa Senators blog guy and one was a Montreal Canadiens guy. If you know anything about hockey, they don't like the Leafs. I knew my market.

Remember when I mentioned negative comments above? Well, if you ever get the chance, go read the comments on that page. You'd have thought I shot somebody. You'd have thought I had shot the Queen. And I quote, "How dare you break up with the Leafs?!" And I reply, "Dude, I'm joking! I didn't actually have dinner with the hockey team. They're not really in my kitchen right now."

What were the results of the video? To begin with, the video has almost 60,000 views. The local news picked it up and put it on television. My mom called me, "Why are you on TV? And why are you breaking up with somebody on TV?" TSN, the Canadian sports network,[126] put the video on their blog. Again, there was no further effort from me. I put it up and sent it to the two bloggers and that was it.

In the end, I did get new viral movie clients from it. Now, at the end of the day, my goal with the video was not to gain new clients. They enjoyed it and liked my style and thought it was fun. I was booked to speak at events because of the video. I also met some local clients from it, too. That's more than I ever got out of the Leafs

---

[125] Here's your little wizard, but don't look behind the curtain—there was no effort involved!

[126] Up here, we call it wannabe ESPN.

in 30 years, so I'm pretty happy with that. Revenue did result from the video, but revenue was not my goal, and earning it was not what measured the movie's success. My goal for this video was simply to just have fun. It was really more of a hobby type of thing.

Back to talking about YouTube. If you ever want to use YouTube video and go against my words, make sure to create a unique domain to point to the video. Because when it said ImBreakingUpwithTheLeafs.com, the URL itself was interesting. People were drawn in by the domain name; it did not just say youtube.6-5/5gg5431. That is not engaging or interesting, it doesn't float my boat. The URL I use is simply a redirect so that when somebody types in that address it simply redirects them to the YouTube URL. This is handy if you are promoting the video off the Internet. I can say, "I am breaking up with the Leafs dot com" on TV or the radio and it sticks.

YouTube is not a good place to build a list. The only option is the subscribe button. It is weak at best. As a visitor to the site, you barely see it. It is difficult to engage with your YouTube subscribers, and you cannot really e-mail them. You can message them on YouTube, but they only get it when they log in. So your conversion rate on the "subscribe to a video" button is really low.

YouTube is filled with competition. You are basically putting your video on a supermarket shelf with better products around it! You have absolutely no control over where viewers will go, not to mention they can easily scroll up an inch or so and see another 18 million videos. You are not controlling your message on YouTube.

Your goal needs to be focusing your viewers' attention and pulling them into your funnel. You can use a squeeze page, which is pretty much a landing page, but has the video right on it, with the goal being for you to watch the live video and subscribe either during or after watching it by using a form right beside the video.

The squeeze page allows you to focus people into the focus funnel. As I have said, YouTube is fine, but you need to use it the right way. You can use the YouTube embedding code and embed it into your site or embed it into a squeeze page. Own your video—remove the part where it says, "suggest other videos" at the end. You will still have the YouTube watermark, but you can own it. You can bring them toward it. Like I said, views mean nothing. It just makes you famous in your own mind.

A great example of how you can take views and pull that audience into your funnel is my motivational site, Thank Goodness It's Monday—TGIM.[127] Once you are in, once you're watching, you've got nowhere to go, sister, nowhere to go except one way. Either get out, or sign up. No other videos of people who are better looking than I am. No other videos that have better words than I do. You're just with me. I converted 38 percent of people who watched my video into a sublist of mine. I've got 14,000 people on that sublist who want to see these exact videos. That is huge! A huge, huge difference. Sometimes the problem with video is that much of the time people get overwhelmed. There's just too much to do. So, you make it simple. There should be nowhere else viewers can go. They sign up or they're done or they pass it along to someone else. It does not take away from the video, and that's what works really well.

One note about video of any kind: If you do a video, even an instructional video, and it is long, respect your audience and tell them it's going to be long. Tell them, "It's an hour-long video and instead of compromising quality, we want to show you this to the best of our ability, so just let it load a bit. In the meantime, go play this penguin bash game or something." I don't care what it is. Tell them if it's going to take a minute. When that loads, please make sure it says "loading" and it gives a percentage so it shows you how

---

[127] ThankGoodnessItsMonday.com/video

soon it will load. If it just sits there and a bar is supposed to go across, you are going to lose people.

Streaming Video

Potentially the most powerful and the most hurtful type of video that you can do for your business is streaming video. It's finally getting to its mass-market point. With high-speed access becoming the norm, and flash technology combined with free streaming sites, it's almost as easy as one click to run your own live TV show. As a matter of fact, if you use a site like Twitcam.com, with just one click you are live. You turn on your camera and the website will let your followers on Twitter know that you are ready to go live. Or using a site like Ustream.com lets you notify your friends on Facebook, Twitter, and so forth.

The biggest problems here are audience and skill. Audience is the ability to generate an audience on the spot for your broadcast. It is tough to get people to do anything at a specific time, let alone for a long period of time. In other words, people take time out to watch your new fancy web show. As an example, even having tens of thousands of followers, on average I will get 100 people watching at any given time.

We have already spoken quite a bit about the challenges of live video—this is 10 times harder in live streaming video because you do not have an opportunity to edit, the comments are live, and you can watch the number of viewers go up and down—all of which are very intimidating.

The best thing to do is to schedule the broadcast ahead of time and notify your subscribers, followers, and friends when it will be happening and then remind them that day. You can also record your live streaming videos. Pretty much all of the live streaming sites will allow you to record the video that can then be embedded into your blog. But be careful the recording does not contain the viewers' questions and comments in a chat form as they do when you are live.

So if you are willing to take questions live, just make sure you repeat the questions on the recording so that viewers afterward will understand what you are answering. Also, one of the bad habits when people do live streams where chat is enabled is that people end up reading the chat while they are on camera and are always staring downward. It looks awkward and you lose the potential connection you get from "looking people in the eye." The best way to handle this is to have somebody else monitor the chat stream for you and highlight key questions to send to you via private chat so your focus can be on engaging with the viewers. I do this with my assistant who sits across the table from me and then holds up good questions for me to read. I keep my focus on the camera and it looks much more professional.

Asking for questions is a great tool, but you need to be prepared ahead of time in case no one asks. It can get awkward when you ask for questions and no one types anything in. So ask your lists, friends, and followers questions beforehand so you can fall back on them if no one asks you questions live.

It really is a great tool. You need to make sure you have comfort in front of the camera and a platform that you have already built so you have an audience to pull from. This is not something for someone new because you will just be talking to yourself.

Social Media

Social media is really good for building relationships and can result in sales if you do it right. Social media is not the best way to build your list. Please let me explain before you tell me that your 5,000 Twitter followers are a list. Basically on Twitter, at any one given time, all of your followers are not sitting at their computers staring at the screen waiting for your message. Only a small segment of followers are on Twitter at a time. You cannot control the distribution of the message to them. You can only tweet and put it out there.[128] I do not use Twitter to build my list; I use it to engage and build relationships. That's cool. That's what's great about social media.

Emotion—How Do You Decide?

Let's take a step back and talk about emotion and choosing this as your goal for your viral project. You need to start by determining one of two things. What are your market's core pain emotions or what are its core joy emotions? What is the emotion the potential customers want to feel or what is the emotion they have right now? Take that and play with it. Find a way to make that emotion motivate them or find out how they could learn from it. For example, if you have business owners in your list or your funnel, one of their biggest issues right now is the economy.[129] That is an emotion—it is fear. You can turn fear into motivation by reassuring them that it can be okay, that they can make it through troubled economic times. Because it can be.

You need to decide which emotion you are going to engage. The *Time Movie* was designed to be inspiring. I knew my audience wanted to be inspired. I knew they wanted to think, and if you make people think, they will want to know more about you.

Be Prepared for Success

Being prepared is so important. This is the most important part of viral marketing.[130] Be prepared for success if it's going to happen.

---

[128] If I tweet something and nobody's there to hear it, does it actually go? I don't know.

[129] Getting freaked out because of the economy, right?

[130] Here's where I start to cry.

Not being prepared for success in viral marketing is worse than never having success at all. Yeah, that's a sound byte, so go ahead and write that one down. You can tweet it. Not being prepared for success is worse than never having success. Has anyone ever had this before? You lose your mind. I know . . .

I was not prepared for the success of the *Time Movie*. My first problem was my server. I had the movie on my own server, my personal hosting account for $9 a month. I'm lucky I didn't put it on a free site like Geocity or something like that from back in the day—the Angelfire days. I put the movie on there, and that's when I learned about the term *transfer bandwidth*. So, the movie goes out. I sent it to a couple of hundred people I had on my own list, and it took off.

The movie takes off! I am a somebody! Then as I am in the middle of congratulating myself, the movie stops working. "Why is it broken? I broke the Internet for crying out loud! I broke the tubes!"

Here's a reenactment:

"Hey, Frank, go see the *Time Movie*!"

"It goes to error 404."

"That's not the thing I'm trying to show you. It's not an error page!"

So I went to my host and told them I was paying a solid $9 a month here! So what the hell was going on? Which is when the rep told me about "transfer bandwidth," which is how much goes from your server back and forth. My limit was less than a gig and at 50,000 views I was capped. Taking the cap off meant that I would be billed per meg. And because I wanted to go viral and show the movie to the world, I agreed! Release the hounds!

So off it went, and the tech rep uncapped it. And it grew— 10,000, 20,000, 50,000, 100,000, 200,000. Would you look at me? I rule! And then I got my bandwidth bill. I went from $9 a month to $1,400, and that was only the last week of the month. I saw the bill and said . . . Well, I can't actually tell you what I said. I looked at my site statistics and I said, "Stop watching the video, stop watching the video, stop watching the video! No more viral. Bad movie, baaaaaad movie! Stop watching it right now."

That is the danger of viral marketing. You cannot stop it. Once it goes, it goes. You can't stop it once it starts going out. Now every time someone watched it, instead of my thinking about the people I was helping, I was thinking about the server. So, I stopped that pain. But, lucky for you, that's not even the beginning.

The next problem was my newsletter list, my subscribers. Oh, my subscribers. I found a way to convert them, that landing page, right? Good? I started my newsletter and I didn't want to pay the $19 a month to host my newsletter. Because, you know, I was already paying $9 for hosting and, you know, that's a lot of money. So I decided just to host the newsletter myself, from my Outlook.

You know, some of you right now are doing that. Don't even think I don't know you're doing it. I just copied and pasted. I had a script, FreeScripts.com, e-mail me anytime somebody wanted to sign up with his or her name and address. I simply went copy, groups, add, paste. Not bad when you get three people a week. When the video blew up and went viral, I was getting 4,000 requests a day—into my Outlook Express. Express? I didn't even upgrade to the real one. I would go to download my mail and it would go, "Oh no you don't." I couldn't download; it would sit there for like 19 hours downloading all the e-mails. And then I still had to cut and paste each one, 12 seconds apiece. So you know what I did? I deleted them. I deleted 140,000 e-mail addresses. That was just in the first couple of weeks.

At this point I was ready to spend some money—you've got to spend money to make money. I decided to put the newsletter on my server and have a script—but then I found a free script! I don't have to spend money to make money after all—free script! I put the free My Mail Script in there. It's an open source thing. The open source community is the most wonderful community in the world. Everybody helps each other. Only problem was that I broke the script! And I had the most open community in the world telling me to get out.

"You are out!"

I said, "You can't, you don't throw anybody out!"

"Except for you."

I broke it. It stopped working. When people would try and sign up they would get an error message. I lost about 50,000 subscribers that way. At that point I finally made the right choice and decided to use AWeber. Pick your poison—Constant Contact, AWeber, whatever you want to use to collect and manage subscribers. I picked AWeber, and I did it and I started crying. Not because it worked, but because I realized how many subscribers I had lost beforehand. I want you to learn from my pain. Please don't cry and make the same mistakes I made.

I don't mean that you need to be prepared for success by having your own dedicated server in rack space in your closet, or a $9,000 a month e-mail plan. I mean be prepared. Have a scalable plan like AWeber or Constant Contact.

We once made a movie for a woman. She loved it and gave us the go ahead. We launched it and she got 12,000 subscribers in 48 hours, and then she got mad at me. She yelled at me. She phoned me up and said, "Scott, what the hell is going on?"

I said, "It's working; that's what we do."

Still yelling, she says, "No, no! It just bumped me to a higher plan on my shopping cart system now. I have to pay $120 a month now."

Seriously, if you can't take 12,000 people (that's what she had in 48 hours) and find a way to make $120 off them in one month, you're doing something wrong. Seriously. Put away your "I'm in business" piece of paper and go work for somebody. Honestly.

I went to her and said, "I don't know what to say."

She said, "Well, do something about it."

"I could turn it off."

"Maybe we should just do that."

I told her she was ridiculous. Why would she not want these people signing up for her newsletter? That was the entire point!

Now back to me:

When the *Time Movie* launched, I didn't have any scalable services. Experts talk about scalable products all the time. I was a speaker, I had a product, and I had me. First thing I needed was a speaker request kit. Two weeks after launching the *Time Movie* I had 50 requests for kits. Remember, I would have been happy with one in a year, and I had 50! But here is the next problem. Do you know how I was putting together my speaker kits? First, I would go to Staples, get the business stuff, get three folders (I don't want to buy the 10, it's too much), put it in, put it through the printer, then my VHS cassette at the time (yeah, I was new), put it in there, fold, bubble envelope, walk to the post office, there's one! And now I needed 50? You know how many I ended up making? Zero. In total, I received about 785 speaker requests before I made the system work properly. I had the golden ring of speaking, and I threw it away! Because I wasn't ready.

You know what I should have done? I should have had a fulfillment center on call. One that charged by piece, so if I got one, I only got charged for one. I don't mean open your own warehouse and get ready. Have it ready. Make it scalable. Fulfillment houses will help you. They print it, they ship it, and you just bring the people in.[131]

Plan scalable products. At the time, I had a CD that was called *Relaxation on Demand*. Pretty cool title. It was two minutes per

---

[131] Ouch, that still hurts me right now. That's two weeks of people saying, "Scott, come and speak." And I said, "No thank you, no, I don't want to, actually. I was kidding." That's what happened.

track for whatever was stressing you out. If driving was stressing you out, you put it on the driving track. So we put it out there on the landing page, available for sale to anyone interested, and it worked! I received 50 orders for CDs in a week.

Do you know how I was making the CDs? Pick up, insert, burn. Fifteen minutes to go. While the CD is burning I print the Avery labels while I'm waiting. Twenty minutes later and the CD is finally done. Then I try and stick the label on the CD . . . and I screw it up! "I need the CD stomper, where is it?" Okay, CD done, sticker on, all together, in the bubble envelope, sealed and all done. It took me 40 minutes per piece.

I sold more than 1,000 CDs in a month. I could not keep up. So I refunded all the sales. I thanked the people for buying my product and refunded their money.

"What do you mean? I want the product."

"No, no, that's fine, just take the refund back. But thank you. Thank you for buying what I wanted you to buy. Please stay on my newsletter? I put you in my Outlook, so you're there."

Do you know how long it takes to bcc 4,000 people? About nine days.

Be prepared! I don't care if it's viral. Maybe it's a program. Automate as much as you can. Make it scalable as much as you can. The TGIM video that I did, the one of me just sitting there talking, led me to do a video coaching program. Not how to make video, but a video of me coaching people on video. Six weeks, sequential, automated. I filmed them once, though, and they're perpetual. The videos can be used forever. That's what I want you to do.

Please learn from my pain. The pain of success stinks if you're not ready for it. Be ready for it. Have things in place. Everybody reading this book could help each other out just by talking about the mistakes you have made and what you have learned. This is one of the best things about Twitter—it is a great resource for good tools.

When I needed a recording program for Skype because I was interviewing for an ebook, I went on Twitter and asked, "What kind of recording program do you use for Skype?" In 30 seconds I had 27 replies.

That's what you need to do. Be prepared for it, because if you are not, it is going to be much worse than not having success at all. By the way, have you ever said that to people who are not successful yet? It's like the worst thing in the world. They hate you. They say, "You sound like a spoiled brat. Don't tell me success stinks." But it does. It's worse because it ruins your reputation. It takes a lifetime to build a reputation and one tweet to screw it all up. Don't do it. Be ready with everything.

So, here's the part where I tell you how we made it right. We have made more than 65 movies total in four years. We made movies that are inspirational, motivational, and funny. We have focused on niche markets such as women, pet owners, real estate, MLM. If you're in direct sales, by the way, it's probably the biggest industry you could get this for. It's all about numbers and building and being scalable. It's huge. Whatever your niche, you can make a movie out of it. I don't care if your market is regional real estate agents in Washington. You can do something. Just do the top 10 ways you know you're from Washington. I just gave you the movie, by the way. It'll work. It'll go. It'll happen.

Our top movie has had 45-million-plus views and more than $5 million in sales. Again, it doesn't stop. It's always perpetual, always comes in, and is always building leads. Fifteen of those 65 movies have more than 1 billion views. Four are my own businesses. And it never, ever stops. The *Time Movie* has never stopped. Think about that for a second. It's perpetual. Right now, somebody just signed up for my newsletter. I'm not psychic or anything, I just know, because it comes in every single day. That, to me, is what business is. Stop trading dollars for hours and start scaling. And viral is a great way to do it, if you do it right.

50

Undercover UnMarketing

I'VE ALWAYS WANTED to be a private eye. Growing up watching the three Ms will do that to you (Matlock, MacGyver, Magnum P.I.). My mission was simple: Visit multiple retail framing stores posing as a customer to do research for an upcoming seminar at an industry trade show. Donning an old baseball cap, T-shirt, and jeans, I set off on my search for the best and worst experiences I could find. Unfortunately, none of the 14 stores I visited could be classified as best because they all performed miserably. My initial thought was that some stores would get it right, treat me as a valued potential customer, understand how relationships equal good business, and that others wouldn't have the time of day for me.

Each store had the same scenario presented to them—a young man in his street clothes comes in to inquire about getting his college diploma framed, which he did not bring along. So off I went, and that's where everything went downhill. I can't really choose which part was worse, the store owner/operator who peered out of the back room announcing "Can I help you?" in a tone that would define "stern" or the rolling of the eyes when I mentioned I didn't bring the item to be framed with me.

At every stop I was told that I should have brought in the piece to be given a proper estimate, and to come back with it if I wanted a quote. Is this reasonable? Of course, I understand the concept of not being able to quote on something you can't see, but there is no need to make a customer feel stupid about it. I was in your store, you've got me through the door, what can you do to make sure that when I leave, I will come back later?

I certainly can tell you what *not* to do:

- **Don't let me off the hook when I say I'm "just looking."** This is the biggest lie in the retail world. The majority of the time, no one is just looking. People don't randomly end up in your store and become curious as to what is inside.[132] Your store is called a *framing store*, not exactly something that draws an "I wonder what they do, let's go inside and take a look!" Especially if you're in a strip mall, people don't just drop in. Even if it's because people really enjoy looking at the art inside, they're expressing interest in what you and the artists do, so capitalize on it! If the person enjoys looking at art, offer to invite them to an exclusive preview of new pieces down the road, or discounts when new pieces arrive. Make them feel special.

- **Don't hand me a frequent shopper card.** I have so many frequent shopper cards in my wallet that it's starting to resemble a new appendage. Instead of making people add your punch card to the masses they already have, offer to keep it in the store and when they come back again, they can let you know they have a card, and they get their discount! Also, make it easy for them to get the incentives if they buy enough. One of the department stores I used to frequent made it harder to redeem my already earned points than it would be to frame a poster by just

---

[132] In a mall this happens all the time, but most of these places are stand-alone retailers.

using Saran Wrap and twigs. The last thing I need is to jump through hoops just to give *you* more business.

- **Don't ask "Can I help you?"** Being of the male gender, the phrase "Can I help you?" sets off the same alarm bells as when I'm told to ask for directions. Something deep down inside tells me, "You, man, need no help . . . grunt." No one ever needs help, but everyone is interested in being acknowledged.

- **Don't wait to acknowledge me.** I'll be the first to admit, I've always had the dream of being the invisible man, but not when I'm in your store. At least six of the stores I visited, the owner was speaking to someone else and never acknowledged my presence until she was done with that customer, plus whatever else she was doing. All it takes is, "Hi! I'll be with you in just one minute," said in a pleasant manner. Therefore, I don't feel like I'm rudely interrupting you when I walk into your store.

- **Don't send me to look at your online brochure (er, website).** The majority of framing store sites I looked at after leaving the store (that's if they even had a website!) were practically the same as their store brochure, except in digital format. The function of your website should not just be to inform, but to collect information about your visitors. Set up a newsletter that says, "Sign up for our monthly newsletter to be the first to see new prints, and receive a 10 percent discount on all future orders." Therefore, you do the "pull and stay" with all of your visitors.

Every single store I visited had an opportunity to engage with me and potentially earn my business. Never mind that if I became a satisfied customer, there would be potential business from those I could recommend to also use their services. The stores could have done so much better. First, store employees need to treat each customer with the respect and treatment that they would use if they were your dream customer with money to burn.

Many store owners I spoke with after the speaking engagement expressed that they really want more corporate accounts, some of which require them to get in touch with a human resources (HR) manager to get the sale. The HR manager is the one who is in charge of incentive plans such as framed prints. Little did these storeowners know, but the guy with the baseball cap is good friends with at least 12 HR managers in the area, and was a former one himself.

As I wrote this section of the book, I actually received an e-mail from a colleague in human resources asking for some opinions on incentive plans. Do you think I'll be sending that person to one of those stores anytime soon? You must view every person who walks through your door as one person removed from your ideal client, and treat him or her as such. I am not an interruption to your day, I am not an inconvenience, I am a potential customer, and a word-of-mouth machine that can spread the word, good or bad. You choose. At every point of engagement, you are marketing your business.

A typical framing store owner practices a push-and-pray technique. People come into their store, look around, and leave. The employee has made no attempt to find out what the shopper was interested in and offered no opportunity to give the store's contact information. The stack of business cards and brochures on the counter, if someone cared to take one, was the standard fare. The owners were defining the term *push and pray*—they were pushing out their marketing (biz cards, brochures) and praying someone would buy from them some other time.

Instead, as mentioned previously, they should be using the pull-and-stay technique. This could be a simple request to gather the potential customers' information through either a contest (giving away a postcard-size print, etc.) or a discount. They could have gathered each person's information and kept in touch with them consistently, so when the time does come to purchase a painting or get something framed, the store owner would be at the forefront of the buyer's mind. One of the easiest methods I've used is to create the "Top 10" list article. Pick the need you fill, the problem you solve, and write an article that would be similar to advice you would give to a customer. We are going to talk about this much more in the section about creating new products.

It's always easier to write a "Top 10" list like this when you choose a focus market. Notice I didn't say a target market. When people think of a target market, they make it far too vague or wide to work (i.e., my target is people who want framing done!). You need to pick a focus that you can get your mind around and meet their needs. Is it new corporate accounts? Local artists?

Once you choose who the focus market is, write your Top 10 list. It could be the "Top 10 Ways to Preserve Your Art." Something your market is interested in. You write the article, print it out, and offer it to every single person who walks in your door. Then you let people know that if they want more information, to give you their contact information and you'll send them new articles as they come out. Now you can be in front of potential customers with great information. And when they have a question about your industry, you are going to be the business they turn to.

No matter what you sell, when you're faced with competition from a bigger store, you tend to look at what you can't do better than them. Small stores can't usually out-advertise big stores or give better discounts. You need to change this focus. Your passion for your craft and the ability to give personalized customer service are the kinds of strengths that smaller businesses should be focusing on and improving rather than worrying about not being as big as your competition. No larger store can send out quality articles periodically to interested potential customers. A big store cannot buy that level of engagement through a television commercial or billboard.

So, what could these 14 store owners have done to get my business? Instead of scolding me about not bringing in the diploma, the owners could have showed me some typical sizes and framing set-ups for my diploma, but with the stipulation that if I could bring it in, I could get a much better estimate. They could have asked what school I went to, get to know me, and begin to build the relation-ship, or handed me a list of ways that I could best preserve my keepsake. Do anything to show that you are interested in my po-tential business with you rather than treating me as an interruption to your busy day. If you're too busy to deal with customers, you should not be in retail.

My diploma is still unframed and in my closet, so I'm off to try some more stores. Now where did I put my cap?

51

Putting It Into Practice

AFTER SPEAKING AT the framing gallery conference, the owner and manager of a small store hired me to consult with them on what they could be doing differently to increase their sales and engage their market. It was a stand-alone storefront in Toronto that carried beautiful pieces of art along with incredible framing services. Great store, beautiful products and services, but still they were frustrated and so I let them vent.

"People come into the gallery and most of them say they're just looking when I ask if I can help them! Now I have to stand around while they browse and they end up leaving. Or they come into the gallery looking for bargains instead of wanting to buy the high-priced original pieces! What can we do to change that?"

The first thing I asked them to change was their mindset. They viewed most people coming into their store as interruptions, instead of someone raising a hand, expressing potential interest. Next I pointed out the LARGE NEON SIGNS in the window advertising "50% OFF!!!" as to the reason why the bargain hunters showed up.[133]

---

[133] Seriously, half the art in the window was obstructed by the ALL CAPS sales posters.

We sat down and categorized people who came into the gallery who were "just looking," then we set up a system to try to pull and stay with each group:

■ **People who liked a specific artist's style.** This specific gallery had a few artists who had exclusive pieces at their gallery. They were magnificent. Some of the pieces I would be interested in purchasing myself. They were the main draw that people could see from the window, if they could see around the "SALE" signs. The job now was to set something up so when they identified that desire, you could make them feel special and exclusive. We decided on a VIP list program where they would approach the customer and say, "He's an exclusive artist with us. We occasionally do private showings and parties with him for our VIP list. Would you like to add your name to the list?" In the first week alone, they signed up 50 people who didn't exist as customers before.

■ **People who liked the idea of art, but wanted the bargain.** Same idea as above. Instead of despising them for buying the low-margin, bargain-bin prints, we played off the desire by creating a sale e-newsletter. Anytime a big sale was coming up, these bargain hunters would be the first to know. Twenty-five people signed on in that first week, and hundreds more in the following month.

■ **People who were curious about art in general.** This group was curious about everything from what type of pieces went with the house color scheme to how to get into the investment side of art. These customers were handed an article about the ABCs of art collecting and care and asked if they wanted to receive a monthly newsletter with more tips and featured pieces. Two hundred people in the first month ended up on the list.

For each group, a small card was created for the person to easily fill out, asking for his or her name and e-mail address. For the exclusive list, the phone number was also requested, because the parties would be small, and it was first-come first-served.

Initially, the owner didn't want to do any of these methods for many reasons. She didn't want to write multiple newsletters or e-mails, and she had tried the wine-and-cheese parties before and they didn't work.[134] The owner had a lot of downtime during the weekdays, so I convinced her that writing a newsletter to her potential customers was not a bad way to spend her time. She needed to position herself as an expert in art, not just a retailer. A retailer wants to sell you something, but an expert advises you along the way.

When it was time to throw the exclusive artist showing party, the owner was not going to just send an e-mail asking the list to attend, she was going to send a nice invite in the mail, which was then followed up with a phone call. The invitation included all the information needed about the event, stating when the party was, and asking if the customer and a guest would like to attend. The gallery could only hold 50 people, so they were asked to commit on the phone.

The night of the party arrived, the gallery was packed, and the owner sold $60,000 worth of art. There were bidding wars, and many pieces were sold that weren't even from the main artist who was featured. Just looking? More like "possibly buying down the road."

---

[134] Their response was, "All we had was a bunch of wine left over." Which lead me to think, "And this is a problem, how?" and "Who ate all the cheese?"

52

Lush

SALESPEOPLE ARE SO important. They need to be engaging with potential customers, not just taking money from people who are ready to buy right now. Salespeople are the front lines, the foot soldiers. The retail associate is the person who is your most frequent point of engagement with your potential customers. They are marketing every single day to people on behalf of your company. They are the most important people in your UnMarketing cycle on a daily basis, and yet they are the number-one reason why sales are lost.

To prove this point, I hopped into undercover mode again and went to one of my local malls to see who would care that I was in their store. It was a Tuesday afternoon, a dead time in retail, so I wouldn't get lost in the crowd. I walked into 20 different stores and felt the same every single time: unwanted, interruptive, and a general pain to the workers who were trying to get important things done like stocking shelves, chatting with each other, or working on their stink-eye look.

And then there was Lush. I noticed this soap store on steroids, because I caught a whiff of it 50 feet away. I really had no need to go into it, because I'm a guy and buy my soap by the truckload in bulk, using it occasionally. But I went in, wanting to round out my day of uselessness of trying to prove that a store could get it right.

As soon as I walked in, I knew I had found that mythical place. Jessica perked up as soon as I walked into the store and greeted me like a long-lost friend. "Hey! How are you? Welcome to Lush! Have you been here before?" I looked around, trying to see if she was talking to someone else, not really sure how to react. "Umm, no, I've never been in here before." She then jumped. "Great! That means I can give you the grand tour! Come here!" Now you have to picture this store—it's maybe 500 square feet—but she gave me a tour that was fit for a palace. She told me about the different sections, why some soap was sold by the pound, cut out of large cakelike slabs, and showed me what bath bombs, salts, and aromatherapy soaps were all about. I walked out of there with $65 worth of soap and a smile on my face. She got it; Lush got it. She engaged with me. She loved the product,[135] and she knew about it.

I now smell like lavender, my skin feels softer, and I am a huge fan of a store I didn't even know existed until that day. Do you think this story would have played out differently if the associate was on the phone, didn't care about me, and just said, "Can I help you?" I think so, too.

Note: I've gone to multiple locations, and everyone who works there has the same contagious energy. Even when I said on Twitter that I was writing about the soap store that rocked my world, someone replied back, "It has to be Lush." Well done, Lush, well done.

---

[135] If you don't love the product/service you're selling, why would a potential customer?

53

Trade Shows

Trade shows are a great opportunity for engagement. You get lots of customers in one place and can put your best foot forward. You have a chance to connect with potential customers and promote your brand. The problem is that many vendors, like sales associates in retail, don't understand that simple body language and attitude can make or break potential on-the-spot sales. It's awkward to approach a booth with the rep sitting in a chair. It reminds me of seeing Santa Claus at the mall for the first time. Unless you want me sitting on your lap, stand up.

I get it, trade shows can be really tiring, especially in the later days of the show. The long days on your feet really can wear you down. But you need to remember that at some shows the buying decision is made on those last few days. Even though you have seen hundreds or even thousands of people go by, this may be the first time a buyer has seen you, so your first impression is still important.

A few months ago, I was speaking at an event and decided to hop over to the trade show exhibit area to see what was around. Although that was not really the reason for my being at the event, I also happen to be a part of their target market. This was the second-to-last day of the trade show, and it really showed. You could tell that most of the vendors were just looking forward to getting home. It does not make a good impression when you leave early or stay physically but refuse to give any more attention to the attendees. Imagine coming to my house for a party I'm throwing and spending all of your time looking at your watch. If you don't have time for me, then I am not going to have time for you.

I checked out maybe 55 booths that day. Of the ones I passed, about five of them had people working inside who looked like they wanted to talk to me, and those were the five I made an effort to really go into and learn about what they were selling. There was also a sixth booth that I tried to engage. The two guys running the booth, both sitting down by the way, made it look like I was interrupting their conversation! I guess because I was. I had the audacity to be curious about what they were representing. They happened to be there to promote another event for the same industry that they were in charge of organizing. Let's just say I no longer looked into their event. Before that day, it was an event that I already potentially wanted to attend. They lost me.

I know one of the nice things about industry events and trade shows is that you get to see people you know from other companies, current customers, or friends in general. But when you're there for sales and the reps in your booth are all talking to each other and they partly form a circle, they make the booth feel like a closed group. Many, many people hesitate to walk into a booth, let alone try to break into a conversation. Your goal at a trade show initially should be to make your space as welcoming as possible for potential customers, so that they walk off that middle aisle carpet at the trade show or event into your overpriced booth carpeting.

You don't do that by having your backs to people or by talking to each other. You do that by having a welcoming look on your face, a smile, and being open to everybody who walks in. If you start to judge me even before I get to your booth, I am going to judge you as well, and it is not going to be pretty. And nowadays, when people can add something to Facebook or Twitter in an instant, your giving someone a cold shoulder could have instant ramifications online, especially with the use of conference hashtags.

During my third and final year at college, I decided to attend the trade show that accompanied the annual human resources conference in Toronto. On my badge along with my name was the ribbon that stated I was a student attendee. In other words, please ignore me, I assume, because it meant nobody was giving me the time of day. I would walk down the middle aisle between vendor booths and get the fake smile from the sales reps who were standing there, as they let their eyes slide down to my nametag for them to qualify whether they should talk to me. When they noticed the red ribbon that mentioned student, their fake smile went away, and they literally looked disgusted or they simply turned away and looked for the next person walking toward them.

One of the things I was interested in was the computer software that we use in the industry, commonly referred to as a Human Resources Management System (HRMS). I was interested because being both a computer geek and going into the human resources field, I knew this was something I had a leg up on when I got into the industry. There were four main providers of this type of software at the trade show. Three of the vendors were almost trying to prevent me from even going into their booths. They seemed to be protecting their expensive high-gloss brochures from me, someone who they felt had no value to them as a customer at that time. Sales reps at the fourth booth were different. They were simply happy to see me and more than happy to tell me about their software.

Please don't forget that I do understand what it's like to work a booth at a trade show. As soon as you commit to talking to one person, you potentially lose the opportunity to talk to somebody else who is peering in at your booth. But your booth at a trade show is the point of engagement. You need to treat everybody like they have a potential influence in the sale down the road, because in reality everybody in one way or another could, including me on this day.

Fast-forward eight months: I was now working in the field, and you'll never guess whom my employer asked to help recommend a new HRMS system for them. That's right, they asked red ribbon boy! And I'm sure you can figure out which system I knew really well because of the engagement I had with a vendor at the event. We ended up purchasing the system, and after all was said and done, the sale was worth more than $100,000. Not bad for a student who had no buying power at the time.

You never know who somebody really is and who they might be down the road. You never know who someone knows currently or who they are going to be meeting with or speaking to after the show. If you believe in the six degrees of separation angle, then why aren't you treating every person you come into contact with at the trade show as somebody who could help your business?

The same thing can occur not only at a B2B industry trade show but at consumer-based shows. You need to evaluate your biases and how they are affecting who you engage. When I write about social media a little later, you'll see how the ability to share customer experiences online is changing who the influencers are. You need to pay attention.

Here's a great example of how prejudice can affect your trade show results:

About 10 years ago, my husband and I went to a woodworkers' trade show in Norfolk, Virginia. He wanted to look around for new ideas. As we walked through, all the company reps talked to him, and practically ignored me. Dave had just burned out his fourth scroll saw, which we had been buying from Home Depot. The show had reps from all the high-end companies with scroll saws for the intricate woodworking. The reps were all eager to show Dave the saws, and how easy they were to use. I don't think that they realized that I did a lot of woodworking as well, although I'm not as talented at the intricate stuff.

When we were talking to the rep from Hegner, he invited me to try the saw, and showed me how easy it was to use. He actually guided me through cutting out a compound cut minia-ture reindeer, while he told me to notice how little vibration the saw had, and other important points, such as how quick it was to change blades and adjust the tension. When we were done cutting out the reindeer, he asked us what we thought. I surprised my husband by telling the guy I'd take one. It was a $1,500 saw; Dave about fell over!

I made it a point to let the rep know that he was the only one who had taken the time to include me, a point I also let his company know. Being the sort of person I am, I also let the other three reps know that they had lost a sale by not talking to me. Ten years later, that saw still works just as well as when it was new, and the company's customer service is excellent! (We had to replace a plastic knob that cracked.)

Lisa Penosky

Puparazzi! Pet Bow-tique

Vendors complain a lot at trade shows about the quality of attendees. They get angry when a certain amount of them don't have immediate buying power at a show. But they forget that many purchases are still trust-based, and the trade show can be a great starting point to build relationships with people.

I know people, myself included, who delay a buying decision at a trade show simply because they haven't seen everything there yet. There are tons of reasons to delay a buying decision related to the trust gap we spoke about earlier. Your company may be new to me, and I want to check with people I trust, or because I still have stock from another company that I need to clear out, or because I need to budget against other purchases. None of these reasons mean that I will not be ready to buy from you at some point in the future—so why ignore me? When I worked the booth at various trade shows as a national sales training manager, I heard these kinds of replies from potential customers all the time. That maybe they would come back later, or give us a call, or let us know another time.

Similar to the art show example earlier, as an exhibitor you need to create not only an effective pull-and-stay method for trade shows, but your follow-up system has to be engaging and almost immediate. It doesn't matter what system the trade show group has given you to collect leads. You can be from the old-school style of simply collecting business cards from potential buyers all the way up to the fancy machines where you can scan their badge immediately and get all of their contact information. The pull part of pull and stay is already done for you, but here is where you can separate yourself from the other vendors at the show. Follow up quickly and personally. And by quickly I don't mean when you get back from the show five days later. I mean have a system where you can get in touch with them within 24 hours. Give them a quick phone call or e-mail them a brochure—pretty much all your leads will come with an e-mail address.

The goal here is to drop them a line to say thank you for coming by your booth. Let the potential customer know you will be sending the materials they requested (if they did) and then start another level of engagement with them. You can do this easily by asking them an open-ended question. Not one of those sleazy sales ones like, "When do you think you'll be ready to make a purchasing decision?" A simple one like, "What did you think of the show this year?" Something like that will start a dialogue between you. I don't mean that you should ask the phony "How are you?" People ask that question every day and do not care about the answer. I mean to ask a question that you genuinely want to know what they thought. I guarantee that you'll not only get responses back and open a channel of post–trade show communication with them. You are also going to get responses from people telling you how impressed they are, about not only the speed of your response to them, but also your personal response to them.

Here is how you get started. If you have fewer than 25 leads to set up this system, you need to go back to your hotel room for an Internet connection or use one at the actual trade show if it's available, so you can e-mail them that day. Just delay going to the trade show bar for a half-hour or so. Trust me, you can do it. You may even run into some of your potential customers at the evening events, and they have already received your e-mail on their Black-Berry or iPhone. I've actually had people seek me out to say how impressed they were that I had already gotten back to them. Pay close attention and remember if a potential customer asked you a question at the show that you couldn't answer just then and send that answer in the first e-mail. Even if they asked you about products or services that you don't offer, recommend other vendors who do. Being helpful in this way greatly endears you to that person.

Some trade shows make it easier for vendors to pull information from attendees than others. At B2B shows, it is common for people to give up their information quickly because they are so targeted. This means that potentially most visitors really do have a serious interest in many of the vendors. When it comes to consumer-based trade shows, it's much harder to get people's information because there are a variety of industries in the booths, making the audience less targeted.

Consumer shows also have more freebie seekers.[136] It's sometimes pretty hard to get people to commit their information.

---

[136] I didn't realize freebie seekers were so predominant at conferences until witnessing it at a carwash/gas station trade show. My friends at Launch Gum had to protect their gum or people would swipe it!

People are often more interested in hitting every booth possible for free samples than actually getting to know you or your product. So you have an even smaller window to engage with the people.

Lisa McDonald, who is the cohost of MeFest, a lifestyle/pampering consumer show that occurs in Kitchener, Ontario, says to vendors:

> Having freebies at the tables is better than having items in a door gift bag because it gives you an opportunity to speak directly to that *potential* client. *Offer* them the freebie. It gives you eye contact with the person and a chance to start the conversation. *Tell* them that if they fill out a ballot they have a chance to win a prize. This then furthers the conversation about the products/services and they will be at your table for an extra few minutes to fill out the required info.

In regard to the giveaway, I remember the big packaging trade shows I used to work. There was almost a scavenger-style hunt for the best trade show swag. One year in Chicago the best giveaway was a cool-looking walking stick from a company (I can't remember their name)—and there's the problem. If you make your giveaway not relatable to your company, then what good does it do for you after the conference? I don't have the exact statistic, but I think the number of people who make purchasing decisions based on receiving a coffee mug is 0.1 percent with a margin of error of 0.1 percent.

Why give away some golf shirts or fancy travel mugs to current customers when that is what they are expecting anyway? And everyone else is doing the same thing. If you give something away, why not give away something that shows the amount of value you provide. Give away a CD or DVD showing your ability to educate that end-user or customer. Make it something you can send to them instead of giving it to them to put in their conference bag, which they will never ever go through entirely. Your pull-and-stay action here would be to say, "At the show this week we are giving away free access to our online workshop and how you can do scrapbooking better. If you give us your e-mail address, we will send you access to it online as well as our free monthly newsletter, which will give you deals on scrapbooking supplies and will let you know about future events." Just like when we were talking about follow-up earlier—get your gift to them as quickly as possible! Then do a potential follow-up e-mail or call a week or so later to find out if they've tried it and start that conversation again. Don't get lost in this sea of conference swag that will end up costing you a lot of money with little return.

54

Social Media at Trade Shows

ONE OF THE great ways to build potential engagement and traffic at your booth during a trade show is by using social media tools before and during the show. The first way to use a site like Twitter for a trade show is to find out if the show has a hashtag. You remember that a hashtag is the phrase with a # in front of it that you can search and find out if other people are talking about it, too.

Go to the trade show website and see if there is a mention of it. If you have a following on Twitter, you can ask the people if anyone knows it. If you don't find a mention, contact the people who run the show, and if they say there isn't one (or ask you what a hashtag is), create one yourself. Pick a short phrase, usually an acronym, and add the year. For example, at last year's BlogWorld conference, the hashtag was #BWE09. This hashtag allows you to go on your iPhone or BlackBerry or Twitter.com and see what people are saying about the conference.

You can search this hashtag to interact with people who will also be at the show. You can do this with people who will be attending and also with other vendors. It is amazing what can come out of new relationships with other vendors! When you engage with other vendors before the show, not only can potential business partnerships develop, but it can make the show much more enjoyable when you know other people with booths. They can do everything from bring your lunch when you're the only person running your booth to potentially watching your booth while you run to the bathroom. There's nothing harder in a trade show than to be a one-person show at your booth, but it's a little bit easier when you can find a few friends beforehand to rely on each other.

Now if you start to see conference chatter on Twitter with the hashtag, this isn't an invitation to spam everybody who's going by saying in all caps "COME SEE US AT THE SHOW!!" You need to use the same engagement principles that you would use during normal interaction on Twitter. Start talking to them in a conversation and ask them if it's their first time at the show. Give them some suggestions as to what parties they should go to afterward. Whatever it is, get the conversation going and engage with them.

Another fun way to use Twitter during a trade show is to have contests that are live. Tweet something like, "The first person to come up to our booth wearing a red shirt and saying the phrase, 'I saw this on Twitter,' wins a free iPod nano," or something. Do that once a day and you get a nice amount of buzz going if your conference and attendees are Twitter-friendly.

55

UnNetworking
Why Networking Events Are Evil

LAST MONTH I attended a local networking event that made me realize the difference between old- and new-school networking. It happened all within five minutes, all at the same Table I was standing beside.

Old School: A real estate agent, with card already in hand, walked up to me and introduced himself, shoving his card at me. I replied with my name and asked why he was giving me his card. His reply was, "That's what we're here for, to exchange information, to network!" I told him I didn't have any cards and proceeded to then listen to him talk about his website and how if we gave him our cards that he had a section where he would post a link to us and in return we could post one for him on ours! Ta-da! Sigh.

New School: Three minutes later, I recognize Danny. Since I've been talking to him on Twitter for months, we're like old college buddies and I give him a huge hug. No awkward "So what do you do?" questions with elevator-speech answers. No card exchange. Just a genuine great feeling of meeting somebody in person who you feel you already know—because you already do.

Going in cold to a networking event is like showing up for a dance at a high school you just transferred to, except at this dance, you have a stack of business cards in your hand and pass them out to everyone. It's awkward, intimidating, and a huge reason that many people who are even the slightest bit introverted don't go to them.[137] And if you come in late, you're screwed. The circles have been formed, people have been bonding for an hour, and now you have to try to ease into a talking circle, not knowing any of the inside jokes.

Going in warm to an event is like a high school reunion. People instantly recognize each other, you hear a lot of "So great to finally meet you!" and hugs all around. And it's so simple to go into an event all warmed up. Twitter is my warming platform of choice. A few weeks before an event, I search the hashtag[138] on Twitter. You can do this for a networking event, conference, anything really. One popular tag is #SXSW, which is the big annual interactive conference in Austin, Texas. Search it anytime and you'll see people talking about it. Since I'm going to it, I search the tag, see who is talking about it, check out their profile, and if they seem interesting, I strike up a conversation. Next thing you know, the conference is here and I spot them across the room, rush on over and say hi. That's new-school networking. The event isn't the introduction; it's the escalation of the relationship.

Going in cold, old-school style to an event is a huge risk. You usually run into one of four types of people:

1. *The Great One:* The Wayne Gretzky of networking events. He or she knows everyone, works the room like a ninja, and makes

---

[137] Even someone like me, who is an extreme extrovert, has no desire to show up.

[138] A hashtag is a term used on Twitter to track an event or topic. Use a # before the word. For example, I'm using #UnBook for this book. Go ahead, search the term at Search.Twitter.com/.

you feel right at home. That person realizes that everyone is there to help themselves and meet people, not to hear about why you think you're great. They listen, sincerely, and make sure to not monopolize all the conversations. This is who you want to be. You don't have to be an extreme extrovert either. Be you, care about what someone is saying, and enjoy the conversations.

2. *The Awkward One:* Someone who comes up to you with a business card in hand, after freshly reading a networking book at home, says a line like, "I'm a professional organizer. If you could organize any part of your life, what would it be?" to the point that the person should just be holding a script in his or her hand. After the initial exchange is done, they stand beside you, sipping something through a straw. They don't walk away, you feel awkward just turning and fleeing, so now you're stuck. No one wants to come over and hang out with you and the awkward organizer, and you almost look like a networking couple.[139]

3. *The Dude with Scotch:* Always a guy, and always with hard liquor, this guy decides the best way to work a room is to get cranked by the bar and start talking like it was a frat party. If your first thought going into an event is, "I wonder how many types of bourbon they serve?" you're doing it wrong.[140]

4. *The Card Collector:* Reminding you of the time you collected baseball cards,[141] this person has a stack of business cards in his

---

[139] I highly suggest the tag-team approach if you must go in cold to a networking event. Pick your partner wisely and get your signals down if you need to be rescued, à la "Seinfeld head-pat" style.

[140] Nothing wrong with scotch, mind you. Creepy guys have just given it a bad name. It should be sipped in a big chair, by a fireplace with a cigar and a silk robe, which is also creepy.

[141] Need him, got him, need him, need him, got him. If you understand that phrase, we will exchange awkward fist bumps in person when we meet. You just jumped up two points on the cool meter with me.

or her hand, ready to rock! The card collector hands them out like the escort flyer guys on the street in Vegas, making sure to blanket the entire room. Sadly, it's usually a real estate agent or insurance peddler who rules this roost. The top of this pile is the one with his or her own picture on the card because someone told them "familiarity creates trust"! This type walks out of the event, counting the number of cards they pulled, and high-fives others with a cheer. "Yes! I gave out all 50 of my cards! Networking is awesome!" Sadly, if this person went back in at the end of the night, he or she would see 47 of them sitting on tables and on top of the bar because people have no use for them.

An exchange of a card should be done after I've met you and we've connected so well that we need to get in touch after the event to continue our conversation/do potential business/give a referral/go bowling. I usually don't bring any cards because of new-school networking. If I didn't get to know you on Twitter beforehand, I will ask you what your Twitter handle is right then and there, hop on my BlackBerry, and follow you on the spot and make a note to say hi online. That's the great thing about new school. You talk before the event, you meet at it, and then talk after online. It's a constant connection before, during, and after.

56

The Awesomeness of Being a 2.0 Author

I DON'T KNOW how authors did it years ago. You pour your heart and soul into a book, it hits the shelves, and you hope people like it. I'm such a spaz, I don't think I could handle the lack of immediate validation and/or rejection. Since UnMarketing first came out, I've been amazed with the immediacy and coolness of tools available for authors. Waking up every day and reading tweets in real time about people loving the book makes me smile. Every. Day.

And they aren't just telling me about it, they're telling each other. It's this passive conversation our readers are having that was untappable (my new word) previously. Sharing every part, from finding the book on their store shelves[142] to their favorite chapters. Discussing ideas and how they are using UnMarketing in their businesses.

As we've talked about before in the book, we need to pay attention to this passive voice. And it's not just on Twitter. Blog reviews and other mentions can happen under our radar. Setting

---

[142] People upload to Facebook and tweet pics of my book on store shelves all the time. It's amazing. Now if they'd just buy it.

up a Google News Alert for your book title in quotes will keep you on top of most mentions online.

The other amazing development for authors today is digital books. Digital books are gaining traction. Do not ignore them. It doesn't matter if you like to read in that format or not. What matters is that your potential audience is reading them. I was initially a little miffed at the Kindle version of UnMarketing because they made all my saucy/sarcastic footnotes into endnotes, and people wouldn't click on them, thinking they were real citations and other ridiculousness, but I now *love* the Kindle version for many reasons:

- *Digital books are easy to buy.* I've had people buy the Kindle version during one of my talks as they're in the audience. This blows my cranium. The drawback of being an author who speaks is when people leave your session, they rush off to the next talk and forget to purchase your awesome book. Or worse, there is no bookstore on site, and if you think that they'll rush to the bookstore when they get home, you're sadly mistaken for the most part. The immediacy and ability for your audience to buy your book on their phone/laptop/reading device in real-time is epic. If you're even a half-decent speaker, the highest moment of intent to purchase your book is during your talk— and people can buy it! Brilliant. (This isn't unique to the Kindle. You can also grab ebooks on the fly from iBook, Nook, Kobo, etc.)

- *Digital books are easy to share.* I freaking love this about the Kindle. You can loan your copy to someone else for up to 14 days.[143] All you need is their e-mail address. You can only loan a book out once, and you can't read it while it's out on loan. I believe it's only available currently to U.S.-based

---

[143] http://amzn.to/UnKindle

purchasers (I'm not sure why they hate Canada), but nonetheless this is great for spreading your content, especially to those who can't afford all the books they want to read. The author/publisher also has to agree to it.

I learned about digital loaning when someone tweeted the link and I retweeted it. I received a large amount of responses that people were impressed I would share that, since it doesn't create sales. I say why wouldn't I? I want people to consume the book, to love it. That's our job as authors as far as I'm concerned. It's not just to write a book or talk about it or even sell it. It's to get people to devour it. I encouraged people to connect on my blog and share their copies and Shazam! We have an UnLibrary!

- *Free R&D.* This actually made me say "Wow!" out loud, which was awkward since I was sitting by myself in a coffee shop, but I digress. Kindle lets you highlight parts of a book. That isn't the cool part. Kindle also takes the data and tells you the most popular highlighted lines from your book.

Highlights

❝ Marketing happens every time you engage (or not) with your past, present, and potential customers.
   Highlighted by 146 Kindle users

❝ If you believe business is built on relationships, make building them your business.
   Highlighted by 121 Kindle users

You can go online and check out the rest of the UnMarketing ones here![144] This is R&D for an author/publisher and tells you what is resonating with your readers. Another great thing to do is to take these and make them tweets. You already know it clicks with people. Bring on the retweets! That's gold, Jerry! You don't have to guess what's working, it's right there in front of you. You can go and check it out for any Kindle book, not just yours. Amazeballs!

---

[144] http://amzn.to/KindleHighlights

Using Amazon Author Central[145] you can log in as an author and see sales info that used to only be available to your publisher. It allows you to track where your book is selling and in what medium.

Accessibility

Audio books open up a whole new audience for an author. From the visually impaired to people who are listening types of learners, there is something about being able to listen to the author read the book that he or she wrote. I insisted on recording my own voice instead of using a voice actor, due to the danger of it being read literally and making me sound like an even bigger jerk than I already do. Recording the book was almost as hard as writing the book. It took four days at MetalWorks Studio in Mississauga, Ontario, which means I now have another thing in common with Guns N Roses, Rush, and Nellie Furtado.[146]

Audible.com makes it available through Amazon, iTunes, or Audible.com. You also get exposure to their lovely subscribers.

And this is only a fraction of what is being done and accessible out there to authors and their fans. Did I mention I did an entire 30-city UnBookTour planned through Twitter without any cost to myself or my publisher? Ya, that too.

---

[145] https://authorcentral.amazon.com/
[146] The first thing we have in common being the ability to rock.

57

The UnTour

I KNEW THAT I wanted a community-based book tour, but I had no idea when it started just how amazing it would be. Over the next few months I would meet face to face with thousands of people from across North America. Every single stop on the tour came from people raising their hands and bringing me to their town, without any cost to me or my publisher. I made my way around Canada and the United States talking with people about UnMarketing.

One of the many cool things about starting the tour in Dallas is that my brother lives there, so we got to hang out. He does sound for bands and events and told me a great story about the band Winger that really helped define the tour for me. They actually played in the same venue I spoke at.[147]

One of the concerns I had starting out the tour was about doing the same thing over and over, and how to keep it interesting for my audience and also for myself. You probably have the same thing

---

[147] Now Kip Winger and I have two things in common: We've played at the same venue and are both fond of high leg kicks during our performances.

in your business. My brother told me that when Winger came and played their show there were only about 20 people watching, but they played like there were 20,000 people. They killed it. And the fans loved the show and gave everything they had back. They could have just said forget it, mailed in a couple shows and walked away, but they rocked it.

I remembered them on every stop: To be grateful for my audience and be more like Winger. It's one thing to say it, but putting a little more Winger into your life and business is hard work. So how do we do it? How do we make stop 1, 9, and 30 all amazing? And how do we make sure to rock every interaction with our customers?

Brand Enhancement

It really is the little things that count. Brand enhancement is something that wouldn't necessarily change your experience if it hadn't happened, but really makes your experience awesome when it does.

I stayed in a whole lot of hotels during the book tour. A bunch of them stood out for me. In North Carolina, the Embassy Suites was a perfect example of how little things can enhance your brand. The Do Not Disturb sign said this, "There are a million reasons you shouldn't knock, if I was awake I'd tell you one." The style and the attitude made me smile. I blogged about it and shared it online the day I was there.

Every day we need to be thinking about how we can add just a little bit of extra awesome for your customers.

Value People

Winger did not take their fans for granted, and neither should we. We spend so much time trying to figure out what's next, and focusing our attention on future customers and growth, that we forget our fans.

Take a good look around and appreciate where you are and what you're doing. Don't neglect people who are giving their time to you. When I tweeted out a picture of the Embassy Suites sign, they replied with thanks within an hour. The reply made me realize they were listening. Just feeling heard by a company can make all the difference.

Real-World Networking

Winger didn't stop meeting their fans. Get off the couch. (I know you're reading this book on your couch.) I love online interaction for the same reasons you do, but nothing beats face to face. Twitter is a wonderful tool for getting to know people before events, so it doesn't feel like a high school dance (at the wrong high school), but you shouldn't stop there. Go and meet people and step outside of your keyboard.

I am so thankful to people who made time in their busy days to come out to a tour stop. The book is just the beginning; meeting people and putting ideas into action are really what UnMarketing is all about. Don't forget, this all started with a tweet: "Who wants an UnBook Tour stop in their city?" You never know whom you're going to meet, and you never know what will happen along the way. Be Awesome.

From Vancouver to Texas, Vegas to Omaha, every tour stop had a different flavor to it. In St. Louis I got to speak at the Duck Room in Blueberry Hill, where I stood on the same stage as Chuck Berry does every month. In Victoria, British Columbia, they created an entire event called *Social Media Camp* and filled an entire auditorium (They win for best tour stop. They're on a frickin island!).

Each city had somebody stepping up to the plate for me. People took risks and took their time to make sure my book got out there. Sometimes people are amazing. Thank you to each and every one of you.

58

The UnEnd

SINCE THIS IS the "UnBook," what would the UnEnd be? Shouldn't this be the opposite? Should this be the beginning chapter? Or a choose-your-own-adventure-style book?

Send an e-mail to UnArmy@un-marketing.com and sign up for the UnArmy, the awesometastic book-owner list so I can send you new sections, videos, and calls-to-action. Oh, and Vegas parties, too, which is the best reason to join.

Let's start a conversation. Say hi on Twitter@UnMarketing or use the hashtag #UnBook to share in the discussions. Find out how others are using the concepts you've just read to better engage with your market and grow your business.

Every day I see examples of the good and bad that companies do. I have the honor of meeting people who believe that good actions mean good business. A few months after first meeting him, I had the pleasure of returning to the Wynn to meet Wes in person, this time to thank him and to see the genuine smile on his face, his humbleness, and the look of true fear in his eyes when I told him I would be opening this book about him. ☺

I want you to join me and unlearn, become unhinged, undeterred, and unstoppable in creating a business that is both successful and natural to you.

This is going to be fun.

Source: Kitestring Creative Branding Studio. www.Kitestring.ca

Acknowledgments

THIS IS THE hardest part to write. Out of 64,000+ words, I'm truly stumped. How the heck do I cover all the people who I'd like to thank; I'm not talking about all the people I've known, but truly the list of those who helped, inspired, and encouraged me while writing this book lists in the hundreds, if not thousands, on Twitter alone who cheered me along the way. But here it goes . . .

To Shannon Vargo, my editor at John Wiley & Sons, Inc., who had the nerve to pick up the phone one day and ask "Why haven't you written a book yet?" To which I could only answer "because I was waiting for you to call." You've been nothing but supportive and encouraging, and you make me feel like you've got my back, which is the total opposite of what I had heard about the publishing industry. And thanks also to Elana Schulman, editorial assistant, and Susan Moran, senior production editor, who had the misfortune of having to deal with someone like me. Your patience and pleasantness was much appreciated.

Thanks to my fellow authors who helped me throughout the process of this scary new world of actually putting words into print: Michael Port, Randy Gage, Kathy Buckworth, Scott McKain, Yanik Silver, Leesa Barnes, Michael Bungay Stanier,

237

Starr Hall, Chris Brogan, Gary Vaynerchuk, Amber Mac, Jay Baer, C.C. Chapman, Ann Handley, The Brains On Fire crew, and Jonathan Fields.

Thanks to my colleagues in the business world, who make being an entrepreneur a little less isolating, and who provided me with undying support and encouragement, especially on Twitter. There are so many to name that I can't possibly begin to list them all, but to name a few: Elizabeth Potts-Weinstein, Allison Nazarian, Amanda Hite, Jenn Wright, Amber Naslund, Summer Boone, Monica Ricci, Leigh Caraccioli, Olivier Blanchard, Amber Osborne, Manya Susoev, Jessica Berlin, Joseph Morin, Brian Clark, Lisa Byrnes, Jo-Anne Wallace, Mat Wilcox, Elysia Brooker, Andrew Hansen, John Morgan, Rochelle Veturis, Missy Ward, Faith Seekings, Dave Fleet, Sonia Simone, Angela Saclamacis. Thank you for being, most importantly, you.

To Alan Weiss and Seth Godin, reading both *Money Talks* (about the speaking business) and *Permission Marketing* blew my mind and changed my brain and started me down this path.

To Laurie Kondo, for putting her neck on the line to give a young, lippy man a chance to teach at Sheridan College. Without you, that dream doesn't happen.

To Sara 2.0, you are the greatest thing since sliced bread. I'm honored to have shared the stage with you, learned from you, and most awesomely, call you my friend. And Debarge is pretty wicked too.

To Alison Kneber, aka Snipey, who runs www.Snipe.net but more importantly gives so much and asks for nothing in return, I owe you the world and promise to keep my WordPress installs up-to-date.

To my longtime friends, who pretty much have no idea what I do all day (i.e., JP told someone I "sell online ads or something"), you're what a guy needs. From the Formerly Famous softball team, to hangin' out and not talking about Twitter, you ground me to a place where I love to be. Thanks Davey, Steve, Annmarie, Jay, Mary, Lukez, Spence, Bush, Casey, and the rest.

To Alison Kramer, who is the best thing that came out of Twitter for me. Your friendship, persistence, patience, and drive for this book to be the best it can be was something of a legend. I'll never forget it and am honored that you're my "besty."

To Karen Livingston, my right arm at UnMarketing, I don't know how you've put up with my madness for all these years, but I hope this book and its success makes it worth it on all levels for you. You help more than you'll ever know but deserve to.

To my family (how to type this while still remaining manly enough not to cry): Mom, you're my best friend and are the reason I have my drive; thank you for being the beacon of our family. My bro Chris, where my stubbornness and smarts come from, I think of you whenever I let the silliness of humans get in my way. To my beautiful sister, Denise, you give more to the world than you could ever get back, including to me. Thank you for being you. To my little brother Dan, you're way too much like me, which is a good thing. Keep being you, my man, there is no one else like it.

To Tammy, my girl, your dedication to me, to this book, and to our family is something that allowed me to get this book out. Thank you for your love, kindness, patience, and for not caring about Twitter. I need that. ☺

To Aidan and Owen, the two apples of my eye, even though by raising you, you're supposed to learn from me, you've both taught me more than the world combined about love, life, and being awesome. Love you both very much.

Index